1 MONTH OF
FREE
READING

at
www.ForgottenBooks.com

By purchasing this book you are eligible for one month membership to ForgottenBooks.com, giving you unlimited access to our entire collection of over 1,000,000 titles via our web site and mobile apps.

To claim your free month visit:
www.forgottenbooks.com/free109401

ISBN 978-1-5282-7607-8
PIBN 10109401

This book is a reproduction of an important historical work. Forgotten Books uses state-of-the-art technology to digitally reconstruct the work, preserving the original format whilst repairing imperfections present in the aged copy. In rare cases, an imperfection in the original, such as a blemish or missing page, may be replicated in our edition. We do, however, repair the vast majority of imperfections successfully; any imperfections that remain are intentionally left to preserve the state of such historical works.

ENGLAND

IN

1835:

BEING

A SERIES OF LETTERS WRITTEN TO FRIENDS IN GERMANY,

DURING A

RESIDENCE IN LONDON AND EXCURSIONS
INTO THE PROVINCES:

BY

FREDERICK VON RAUMER,

PROFESSOR OF HISTORY AT THE UNIVERSITY OF BERLIN, AUTHOR OF THE
'HISTORY OF THE HOHENSTAUFEN;' OF THE 'HISTORY OF EUROPE
FROM THE END OF THE FIFTEENTH CENTURY;' OF 'ILLUS-
TRATIONS OF THE HISTORY OF THE SIXTEENTH AND
SEVENTEENTH CENTURIES,' &c. &c.

TRANSLATED FROM THE GERMAN,
BY SARAH AUSTIN.

THREE VOLS.
VOLUME THE SECOND.

LONDON:
JOHN MURRAY, ALBEMARLE STREET.
MDCCCXXXVI.

LONDON:
Printed by W. CLOWES and SONS,
Stamford Street.

CONTENTS OF VOL. II.

LETTER XXXVI.

LETTER XXXVII.

LETTER XXXVIII.

LETTER XXXIX.

LETTER XL.

LETTER XLI.

ENGLAND IN 1835.

LETTER XXV.

English Civility—Hyde Park—Equipages—Westminster Sessions —English Procedure—Practical Eloquence—Prison—Tread-mill—Political Creed of a Radical—Specimen of an English Family of the Middle Classes.

London, Monday, May 18, 1835.

Mr. T——g introduced me to his father, who invited me to dinner for next Thursday, and offered his services in any way in which they might be useful to me. When I mentioned Waagen to him, who was perhaps to accompany me to Oxford, he instantly extended his invitation and his offers of service to him also. Such traits of manners as this are certainly not piquant dishes *à la* ——; but, at least, they are quite as characteristic as those which he has such malicious pleasure in relating.

There was a countless train of equipages yesterday in Hyde Park — the same in Regent's Park, and God knows where else; and yet, on an average, no one keeps a carriage who has not 3000*l*. a-year to spend. In comparison with the affluence which manifests itself here, the whole continent seems poverty-stricken. Such wealth

VOL. II.   B is very imposing, inasmuch as it is combined with so much industry, and is, indeed, chiefly its offspring. A combination of poverty and high-mindedness may have a very good effect on the stage, but, in every-day life, the union of affluence and high-mindedness is far more "comfortable."

—— ——— the high Tory preacher at the ——— Chapel, complained that I lately talked in a very absurd manner at ———'s about things that I did not understand. From this may be inferred, that others thanked me for the part I took in the discussion. I have been longer in England than he; and twenty-five years dedicated to the serious study of a particular subject give me as good a " settlement" for constitutional law and politics, as a longer residence in London gives to a parson. Just as little has S———'s correspondent become a sage, because he has been sitting, perhaps for years, on a three-legged stool in England. Is it assuming in me to speak thus, or rather to exhort myself to take courage, because I really have none? I do not pretend to know all about the Berlin hospitals, sugar-houses and gas-works, because I have been a citizen and inhabitant of that city for a long time; and yet every one thinks himself an adept in affairs of state, and in the fine arts! If, on the one hand, I feel how little I know, when compared with the really instructed (that is to say, the great statesmen that figure in history), on the other, I feel that I have learned something from them, when compared to the wholly ignorant.

Yesterday Mr. S——— took me into the Court

of Quarter Sessions for Westminster. Often as
these things have been described, by mouth and
pen, and little as there is to be said about them
that has not been said before, yet every impression must be new. I have often found that
once seeing and hearing gives clearer ideas of
certain things than long study without seeing
them;—so I will give an account, in the shortest
possible terms. The room is high and spacious,
and lighted from above and from the side, by very
large windows, which open into another room:
the air is perfectly pure, and every thing neat,
and even elegant.

All matters which do not fall within the com-
petence of the police, and which must be decided
by a jury, but at the same time are not offences
of the heaviest order, are tried in this court. The
evidence taken before the police magistrate is
laid before the so-called grand jury, which decides
whether the affair is to go to a trial or not. If this
has been determined in the affirmative (which is
expressed by two words on the formulary, "a true
bill,") the proceedings begin; if in the negative,
the accused is perfectly free, and cannot be sent
back to the police, or visited with any extraordinary punishment. This function of the grand
jury seems to be performed with great expedition
and brevity. As soon as the accused is brought
up, the counsel for the prosecution states the
case; when he has finished his speech, the accused is permitted to reply. The witnesses are
then examined; and the accused is asked,
whether he has any thing to offer in his defence:

If the jury returns a verdict of 'not guilty,' the accused is instantly set at liberty; ·if of 'guilty,' the magistrates on the bench consult on the punishment, and the chairman pronounces sentence.

The class of attornies and advocates (or barristers, as they are here called) whose characters with us are combined with those of justice-commissaries (*justiz-commissarien*), here appears divided. The former prepare the business, and then place it in the hands of the advocates, but never speak themselves in the courts. In most of the affairs which come before this court neither attornies nor advocates are employed; the parties avoid, all expensive assistance.

This is a slight outline of the course of proceeding. But each case has a peculiar character, and was dealt with in a peculiar manner; and I cannot withhold my preference of these proceedings over ours in many respects. But I must relate to you a few of the particulars on which I found my judgment.

A woman, of otherwise good reputation, mother of four children, steals a piece of meat out of a butcher's shop, in a fit of drunkenness. Punishment, a few weeks' imprisonment.

A worthless fellow,.well known as such, steals a snuff-box of small value. Transported for seven years.

A carman commits an assault on the woman who keeps a gate at which a private toll is collected. To pay 5*l.*, or be imprisoned for a considerable time. He is allowed time to make his choice.

A boy of fourteen steals a pocket-handkerchief. Imprisonment for some months, with hard labour and whipping.

From these and similar cases I drew the following conclusions :—

1. That public procedure furnishes occasion both to jury and audience to sharpen their sense and talents for questions both of fact and of law; and teaches them to estimate the value of a good and impartial administration of justice. This is an education to the full as important as any reading and writing can bestow. The objection, that in this way instruction is given in crime, and an inclination for it engendered, is absurd. Every thing unfit to be heard is avoided; and certainly there is nothing very attractive in the punishment which inevitably ensues.

2. According to the Prussian procedure, every one of these trials would have furnished matter for a thick volume of *Acten*, compiled by some unhappy *Refendarius*, and would have lasted for months. Here it was decided in a few minutes; and not only judge and jury, but even the parties, saw and heard that every thing was satisfactorily examined and investigated.

3. The English, it is said, adhere pedantically to the letter of the law; but those who make this assertion do not explain distinctly what they mean. The judge here has a far wider discretionary power than they imagine: for instance, when the value of the stolen property is nearly the same, the punishment is very different, in consideration of various aggravating or mitigating

circumstances. This was new to me; and hence
followed,—

4. The correction of another mistake. When
(as is generally the case in Germany and France)
certain punishments are invariably attached to
certain offences, the jury, in pronouncing the
verdict of guilty, have in fact awarded the precise
punishment. The distinction between the question of law and question of fact does not exist:
the one is unalterably decided with the other. If
the jury disapprove the law, they transform themselves into legislators, and acquit (because the
punishment seems to them too severe for the
offence) where they ought to condemn. Thus,
in France, in all trials of women for infanticide.
But in the cases I have mentioned above, the
verdict by no means involved the exact measure
of punishment;—the apportionment of it lay with
the judge, who had thus a peculiar office to fulfil,
and a fair field for a discriminating application of
the laws. There was a heart-rending case, in
which a father had to appear as accuser of his
own daughter, a girl of fifteen, who, after other
profligate courses, had robbed him, and appeared
perfectly irreclaimable. The grief of the old
man at having to accuse his child—the manner in
which, amid his tears, he rather sought to excul-
pate himself, than to insist on the guilt of the
culprit—and, at last, the agony of remorse which
burst from the youthful, and yet apparently
hardened sinner; never did I see or feel any
thing like it! All present seemed to feel their
passions purified and chastised, and to be struck

with so awful an example of human depravity. The sentence was transportation; and Mr. R—h, the chairman, or presiding magistrate, distinctly explained the reasons for this sentence, comforted the father, and solemnly admonished the criminal.

Throughout the whole proceedings, I remarked in Mr. R—h, one while a cheerful, affable, and encouraging air; then legal acuteness and discernment; then gravity and dignity;—always a manner appropriate to the circumstances, but never hard and austere. This practical appropriateness and eloquence the Englishman acquires from his practical life, and from the publicity which accompanies all his actions. He cannot drawl and mumble, and repeat things over and over, in the way which we are unluckily so often obliged to hear.

From the Sessions House, Mr. L—— conducted me to one of the principal prisons. Mr. C——, the governor, showed me every thing remarkable, with the most attentive civility. The main building, with its divisions or dependencies, was built on Bentham's plan: according to which, the governor can inspect the whole from a central point. There was another building which seems to facilitate still more the constant supervision of the whole. Here I saw the treadmill for the first time. Hitherto, the power and motion of this machine have been applied to no practical end: it has been used only as an instrument of punishment: it is more particularly applied to street-

walkers.   There is no want of cleanliness, fresh
air, or wholesome food.

The most remarkable thing in the whole establishment is, that all the prisoners are compelled
to preserve absolute silence.   This order is rigorously enforced by overseers stationed in the midst ˋ
of them ; by frequent unexpected observation, and
certain punishment.   Compulsory Pythagoreans
and Trappists !   I saw above a hundred working
in one room in silence, and twenty washerwomen
washing in silence !   This total privation of oral
intercourse is said to increase the punishment,
and to force every man to reflect upon himself :
at all events, it cuts off the moral infection, in
consequence of which many leave prison worse
than they entered it.

Friday, May 22.

. I began my career of yesterday, after four hours'
work at home, with a visit to Mr. ——, member
of parliament for -——.   I had a great curiosity
to hear the conversation of a man who universally
passes for a most violent Radical.   As what I
said is nothing to the purpose, I shall convert
the dialogue into a monologue, and tell you what
Mr. —— said, with instructive frankness and
readiness, in reply to my numerous questions and
objections.   What was not expressed, or only
half suggested, in an essay on corporations, here
assumed the distinct form of general principles.

After Mr. —— had thrown a glance of sympathy and compassion on the Prussian municipal

organization (of which he knew nothing), and had enlarged a little on the greater progress and higher station of England, even in this respect, he continued in this strain.

The English people have attained to such a practice and dexterity in the business of elections, that these are to be regarded as the true source of all reform, and indeed *of all government.* For this reason I desire annual elections—not only of members of the legislature, but of the magistracy. This is the best means of securing the services of the good, and of getting rid of the bad. It is unnecessary and absurd to allow the government any interference or control, or to give it any central jurisdiction. All abuses, disputes, and uncertainties would be removed by rendering all offices elective. I wish for only one judge in every tribunal: not at all because he has the aid of a jury, but because Bentham has shown that all plurality of functionaries is useless and pernicious in this case. On the other hand, the electors ought to have the power of dismissing the judges at any moment, and without process. This is the only means of securing a good administration of the laws. The right of election is not to be intrusted to any select class or body, endowed with this or that qualification, but to the whole people; and the word *people* includes all, — for there exists in reality no such thing as populace. The whole people thus governs itself: it needs no other government; and all those distinctions and oppositions of sovereign and subject, the source of countless evils, are put an end to at once. The idea ":people" admits of no differences; I reject all qualities; and, with a view to constitution and politics, acknowledge only quantities. Ten is ten, and a hundred is a hundred, and so they will ever remain. I reckon simply with numbers; and it is absurd to attempt to raise or lower quantities by means of qualities. North America is the first and only country which has right ideas on this subject—the only government which has exhibited a pure democracy. The majority decides every question, and always decides aright. There is no other means of ascertaining, developing, and enforcing Right, but by the majority; and, together with the opinions and the expressed will of the majority, Right changes, and assumes new forms suited to each succeeding moment.

These then (I could scarcely misunderstand what was so distinctly expressed) are the principles of a perfect Radical. To these few maxims, which are as easily handled as a Nürmberg toy, does the laborious variety of science and of history reduce itself;—this is the amulet which will avert all the evils and maladies incident to the social structure. With the four rules of arithmetic —nay, with simple addition, which will prove where the majority lies—we can answer all the questions, solve all the problems, which have puzzled statesmen; or, rather, we can show their emptiness and nullity. With one magic word, populace is every where annihilated; or, inasmuch as it forms part of this 'majority,' its empire is established, and its will hallowed. That inconvenient institution, Government, is transformed into the complaisant and obedient servant of the majority; and as a minority is nothing, as opposed to a majority (no matter what their respective qualities), politically and constitutionally considered, it no longer exists. Talent, eloquence, or any other quality, may seek to acquire influence by ingratiating itself with the majority;—for through it, and by its will, must every thing be done; that the fundamental principle of the sole supremacy of the Quantitative may remain immutable and intact. If a unit can contrive to get a certain number of cyphers to range themselves on his right hand, it is well; but if they should choose to stand on his left, he becomes a mere decimal fraction, and falls into the minority. All else that has ever been thought, or invented, or organized, is of evil, and is a departure from the eternal laws of nature.

Remarkable—how nearly this code of philosophy and politics is allied to that of the Abbé Siéyes, and other political teachers of the year 1789,—however different the roads to it appear. As little, however, as a genuine and durable edifice of social relations could be built on the French philosophy which prevailed from Voltaire to Siéyes, so little could one be raised on this superficial doctrine of utility and of numbers. The labours of the greatest men, the experience of centuries, the happiness or misery of many nations, are thrown into a lumber-room; and one has only to put a ready-reckoner in one's pocket, and swear by it (as they do here by the thirty-nine articles), and one is an adept and a prophet.

The antagonists of this school of lifeless abstractions—the high Tories—on the other hand, can never get out of their individual facts for a moment, or take a large and historical view of any subject. But I see what a risk I run of a castigation from both parties, and hasten to take refuge in the security of the middle classes.

I yesterday made the acquaintance of a worthy family of the kind, on which more of the real existence, safety, and prosperity of England rests, than on the warfare of those paper kites which these parties send up into the air.

Mr. T——, an opulent merchant, had invited me and Waagen to dinner, with the most cordial friendliness. Our host was a well-informed, intelligent man, who, with his three daughters, has travelled over Germany, Switzerland, Italy, and France. All spoke German better than I speak English, and had made a treasure of sketches and little drawings, as memorials of their travels, which showed as much sentiment and intelligence as technical skill.

A trio for the piano-forte, harp, and violoncello, was well executed by two of the daughters and the father; and so (you are inclined to conclude) another specimen of over-laboured education, for the purposes of effect and silly admiration. No such thing; these very girls were in the highest degree natural, unpretending and easy in their manners: they united to all these attainments a cheerfulness of temper, resting on religious principles, and on a benevolence which (I have been credibly assured) shows itself in personal attention to the poor. I found myself more at my ease than among Radicals, or than in the loftiest regions of aristocracy.

The same thing is not suited to all, nor good for all; and I am one of the last to wish that all trees should bear the same foliage. Yet one cannot help feeling that, though extraordinary specimens are interesting as natural curiosities, the trees which must compose the forest of the country—at once its strength and ornament—must be like these.

LETTER XXVI.

Visit·to Haileybury—English Sundays—Want of intellectual
Recreation—Want of popular musical·Education—Beer·Bill—
.Beer Shops—Gin Shops—Causes of Drunkenness—Prostitution
—Illegitimate Children—Population—Increased Value of Life.

London, Sunday, May 25, 1835.

YESTERDAY, I went with Messrs. P—— and
P——¯to the East India College at Haileybury,
near Hertford, in compliance with the kind invitation of Pr—— V. S. The weather was perfectly favourable, both going and returning; two
of the loveliest spring days. Horse-chestnuts,
laburnum, hawthorn, lilacs, all in the most brilliant and luxuriant bloom; the whole way a succession of elegant houses, neat cottages, and farms,
—gardens, meadows, fields, richly interspersed
with trees. Passing through Hackney, Stam-
ford-Hill, Tottenham, Edmonton, Wormleigh,
and Hoddesdon, we reached our journey's end in
about two hours and a half. It was hardly possible to say where one village or small town
ended and another began; so thickly sprinkled
were the dwellings, the interval between which
was never greater than was necessary to heighten
the variety.

The East India College was established by
the Company for the education of the young men
destined to their civil service. The course of in-

struction is consequently special. The expenses of the students are not small, (the table, for instance, alone, costs fifty-two guineas a-year,) yet the Company is obliged to contribute a considerable sum towards the salaries of the very well paid Professors. Each of these gentlemen has a pleasant residence and a beautiful garden: the buildings, on the whole, however, can lay no claim to architectural beauty; on the contrary, they display a total inability to reconcile the objects of utility with the demands of art.

On Sunday I arose, while all the rest were asleep, and wandered into a wood of oaks, thinly scattered amidst grass and underwood: spring flowers were under my feet, and larks and other birds singing and fluttering around me,—no other sound to break the deep silence and the perfect solitude. After having for months seen and heard nothing but the restless motion and the ceaseless din of London, this sudden stillness and seclusion had the strongest effect on me: I felt as if there were no human being but myself on earth,—as if I were alone; and, excepting the birds, no other living creature existed. This, combined with my real separation from all my dearest and most cordial friends, and with the dim recollections of all scenes of home and country, threw me into a fit of unspeakable melancholy. But I shook it off and returned back to habitations and to men.

I breakfasted with Mr. J——, and had a long conversation with him on the condition of our agricultural population, and the relation of English farmers and tenants to their landlords. It is only by degrees that I begin to perceive, from my own experience here, how difficult it must be for an Englishman to enter thoroughly into the nature and current of our institutions.

I attended Divine Service, and heard a very celebrated preacher ; looked at the library, and returned home alone, as I was to dine with Lord M——.

So here again were two days full of instruction and variety. If I do not go into more minute detail, it is from the pressure of other labours. But I must indulge myself with an outpouring on the subject of the English Sunday.

I perfectly admit that the English ought to draw a sharper line of distinction, or rather contrast, between the sabbath and the week days, than any other people. After their intense devotion to, and ceaseless occupation about, the things of this world, they need to be more strongly reminded of another, than the Germans and many other nations. People of education, too, doubtless fill this day in a varied and intellectual manner. Nevertheless the contrast of the week-days and the Sunday appears to me too narrow, I might say too Judaical : the cheerful recreation and gladness of mind, which are much more congenial with Christianity than many sects believe, are entirely wanting. The lower classes, who often have to toil wearily through every other day, find Sunday (as it is constantly described) the weariest of all. Often, after serving an austere master, they are made to see in the Father

of Love an austerer still. Singing, music, dancing, the drama, and all amusements which are
addressed to our intellectual nature, are forbidden and denounced as schools of the devil. What
is the consequence? That people of temperate,
regular habits conduct themselves in a temperate
and regular manner; while a great number of
the less sedate and less patient of restraint give
themselves up to the grossest sensual enjoyment,
and seek in that the distinction between Sunday
and working-day. One set of people complain of
the desecration of the Sabbath,—and in this they
are perfectly right; but the only means they can
devise for the remedy of the evil are still severer
·laws; and in this, in my opinion, they are quite
wrong. If (the difficulty of which can hardly be
calculated) all public-houses and gin-shops could
be entirely closed on a Sunday, what would the
common people do then? how would they get
rid of their intolerable ennui?—By spiritual exercises? But are not two sermons, two services of
religion, sufficient? Are they not as much as the
mind of an ordinary man can bear?—By reading?
But many cannot read, and more have not books
which they care to read.—By sleeping; or what?
In this way we should arrive at the conclusion,
that, to avoid all these disorders, some millions of
people ought every Sunday to be chained or
locked up.

I am convinced, on the contrary, that drunkenness would decline, if music, dancing, and all the
less sensual and animal recreations were allowed.
These necessarily impart higher pleasures and

more refined conceptions; or, at least, tend to generate a taste and an aptitude for them. A man who enjoys singing, dancing, or the drama, cannot possibly be very drunk; nor is brutal grossness of behaviour compatible with social recreation.

The utter want of all musical education for the people is doubtless another effect of this way of observing the Sunday; and where this broad foundation for the culture of any art is wanting, individuals seldom rise above mediocrity. It is only on masses susceptible of musical enjoyment, and endowed with musical perceptions, that the lofty superstructure of art is gradually reared, and, from its height, reacts on the mass whence it sprung. I utterly deny that millions of Englishmen are better Christians because they sing badly, or because they do not sing at all. A few London morning concerts, or an expensive Italian opera, have nothing to do with the musical education of a people; and just as little with pure taste, or a true perception of art.

As I have accidentally been led to the subject of drinking, I shall not quit it without telling you something about the new Beer-Bill, which has been so much controverted, and on both sides with some degree of reason. The duties on malt, hops, and beer were so high that it was thought necessary to take off a part, and that on beer was accordingly repealed; partly with a view to lighten the general burthen, partly to procure cheap beer for the lower classes, and thus entice them from the more pernicious spirit-drinking.

A second aim of the law was to put an end to the monopoly of the great brewers; to facilitate the sale of beer by licensing a number of beer-shops, and to deprive the magistracy of the power of favouring a few at the expense of the many. Experience has proved that some of the objects aimed at have been attained, and others completely missed. The monopoly of the great brewers has been destroyed, so far as it arose from their exclusive right of sale; but it remains, of course, so far as it is the result of capital, and of the power capital gives of brewing better and cheaper beer. The consumption has increased, but not sufficiently to diminish the consumption of ardent spirits. On the other hand, the hope of easy gains, and the facility of getting a licence, has called into existence a host of beer-shops, and has caused a proportionate resort to them, and consequent corruption of morals.

It has therefore been suggested, that the price of licences should be raised; that certain securities should be required from persons who open beer-shops; that more power should be given to the magistrates to repress abuses; that the beer-shops be closed at an earlier hour, and that the proprietors be allowed to sell beer, but not to suffer drinking in their shops.

The defenders of complete freedom of the sale of beer pleaded, on the other hand, the difficulty of carrying into effect police-restrictions of this kind, and of enforcing morality and temperance by law.

The consumption of beer has not increased by

any means in the same proportion with that of tea, coffee, and spirits; but the tax during the war was raised as high as 150 per cent. on the value; some diminution of it was therefore just and expedient. It was most unjustly levied on sold beer alone, consequently it fell almost entirely on the poor; leaving the rich, who brewed their own, untaxed.

In the last six years before 1830, the yearly consumption of malt amounted to 32,404,000 bushels:

In 1830 . . to . . 28,844,000 bushels
1831 35,160,000   „
1832 40,344,000   „

In the year 1824 the duties on British and foreign spirits amounted to £5,303,000. After the reduction of the duties in

1825 . . . . £5,786,000
1826   5,474,000
1827   7,492,000
1828 . . . . . .   8,000,000.*

There is no question that spirit-drinking is infinitely more pernicious than beer-drinking. Mr. Buckingham has laid very curious facts on this subject before the House. He asserted that the fourteen largest gin-shops in London were visited, in one week, by

142,453 men
103,593 women
18,391 children
───────────
In all 269,437 persons.

* Hansard, iv. 501; vi. 211, 543, 750; vii. 483; xvii. 270, 702.

XXVI.] GIN-DRINKING. 21

Of these, the women and children had been more
disorderly in their conduct than the men. In
one part of Edinburgh there was one gin-shop to
every fifteen families; and in an Irish town of
800 inhabitants, there were 88. In Sheffield,
thirteen persons came by their death within ten
days, from causes which were asserted to have
sprung out of drunkenness *. An eye-witness
says,—In one part of Ireland the inhabitants are
dirty, ragged, and hungry; they live with the pigs
and sleep upon dunghills. Without doubt this
wretchedness proceeds in part from absenteeism,
from the system of underletting, from high rents,
and, in a less degree, from tithes; but I am persuaded that whiskey-drinking is a greater curse
to Ireland than all these united.

The men too frequently go to beer and gin-
shops, under pretence of getting something to
strengthen and refresh them, and leave their
families to starve. A petition from 220 women
was presented to parliament against these places
of seduction. Lord Brougham declared that
spirit-drinking was a source of innumerable evils
and indescribable misery.

Admitting (as some, I dare say with reason,
affirm) that there is great exaggeration in these
statements, and that, in the middle classes, drinking has diminished instead of increasing, yet the
picture they present is certainly among the most
afflicting of modern times, and the legislature
ought to use every endeavour to eradicate so
dreadful an evil. Increase of duties, prohibitions,

* Hansard, xxiii. 1107.

and 'all mere mechanical external means will effect
little.   The tastes and views of the people must
be elevated; the moral sentiments and the nobler
powers must be awakened and cultivated; and
they must be won from bodily and animal, to intellectual and human, enjoyments.   And so I
come back to Sunday, and to the best mode of
consecrating it to the glory of God and the service of man, from which I started.

Tuesday, May 26.

You ask whether the enormous wealth of England is not oppressive to the feelings of poor travellers.   To this I could answer No, and Yes:
No;—in as far as this wealth facilitates all social
intercourse, and the thought never occurs to you
that certain small expenses can be a burthensome
tax to Englishmen; as they are to many a German,
who ponders long whether he shall buy a bottle
of wine for a stranger or not.   Yes ;—inasmuch as
the great inequality of fortune; even where it does
not lead the poor man into a ridiculous attempt
at rivalry with the rich, yet compels him to think
of a multitude of small expenses, about which it
is not necessary for the rich to lose his time.

*   *   *   *   *

I really think there are not in the whole world
so many prophets of evil to England as in Berlin;
the ' Wochenblatt,' the ' Spikersche Correspondent,' and even the clever, acute observer and
elegant writer of the ' Preusse.'   Great Britain,
according to them, is rapidly and inevitably
dying, not of one, but of ten different mortal

diseases : reform and revolution, taxes and debt, poverty and ignorance, decay of agriculture, excess of manufactures, drunkenness, prostitution, &c. &c. All mere colouring—black upon black— or at the best an extravagant rhetorical Rembrandt.

But, you will say, have not I drawn a picture of this sort respecting drunkenness? Certainly, because I borrowed my colours entirely from the palettes of the complainers. I am far from thinking that figures and sums in addition are infallible; and even if they were, the healthy are far more numerous than the diseased. Since the poor-laws were altered, and the idle can no longer come upon the parish funds, drunkenness has greatly declined. It has never been so bad as in America, where the Temperance Societies are now effecting great good. They will doubtless be of use in England.

May the blessing of heaven rest on every attempt to extirpate this odious vice, here and elsewhere! But why this outcry about England alone? Is Russia a whit better in this respect? It is only in countries where a good beverage is very cheap, as in the south of France, Italy, and Spain, that the people do not get drunk. It does not seem to occur to any body that some approach towards this state of things might be made, by the removal of restrictions on trade, by alterations of duties, &c.; or that it is the imperative duty of governments to employ such measures. Any financial deficiency would be far more than made up by the increase of moral and physical strength.

Another subject with these dark colourists is the number of prostitutes. They are unquestionably very numerous; but when I hear it asserted that there are 50,000 prostitutes and 50,000 thieves in London, with just as much confidence as one states the number of an army, I ask myself, who has counted them? and who knows whether an ' 0 ' might not safely be struck off? Such numbers are generally overstated by one party and understated by another. When we read some accounts, we cannot but believe that London is worse than Sodom or Gomorrah. I have often passed in an evening through those streets which are reckoned the very worst, and there were certainly a number of women about with no very chaste intentions. But the number is not greater than in Paris; and those in London are indisputably more decently dressed than the fair, or rather the ugly, of the Palais Royal. Even if the number of prostitutes be really greater in proportion to the population here than in Berlin, the fact is quite inconclusive as to the greater unchastity. Setting aside the consideration that the distinct and peculiar race of sailors, with their followers, ought to be separated from the regular inhabitants of London (which would make the proportion in favour of this city), there is another observation which is confirmed by many facts. Prostitutes are a distinct, an unfortunate, and, too often, a completely lost class. But the 'contrebande,' which is carried on in private houses and families, is much rarer here than elsewhere; indeed, is almost impossible. In Berlin, where a number of lodgers inhabit one house, and the street-door is always open, not only have the male and female inhabitants of the house great facilities for meeting, but visits, assignations, running out, and so forth, are not attended with the slightest difficulty. Here, on the contrary, only one family occupies one house; the door is constantly shut; every knock, every one who goes out or comes in, is heard, and the master and mistress exercise a strict supervision, or *can* exercise it if they will. A maid servant who is discovered in equivocal proceedings immediately loses her place, and finds it difficult to get another. The race of cooks and housemaids is therefore certainly more chaste and decorous than in Berlin, where many seek unlawful gains, and nobody observes or punishes them, because there is not the slightest reason to suppose that the new-comer will be better than her predecessor.

If a statement I have seen is true*, that the proportion of illegitimate to legitimate children in England is as 1-19, this evil is not greater than in other countries.

*   *   *   *   *

For a time England was the subject of extravagant admiration and praise on the continent, and every institution, every usage, was held up to imitation: now, as it seems, we are fallen into

* Browning, p. 342.

the opposite extreme. I try, at any rate, to steer between this Scylla and Charybdis. There are things which appear to me wrong and defective; but they appear to me, at the same time, susceptible of correction and of improvement.

The notion that an increase of population (without reference to other circumstances) is the greatest blessing of a nation, is now generally and justly rejected; but, spite of the doctrines of Mr. Malthus, I can see no cause for congratulation in its decline. A country like Great Britain, to which the whole world lies open, has, least of all, reason to dread permanent over-population. Indeed, the increase of people may generally be regarded as a sign of the increase of demand for labour, and of means of subsistence.

The population of Great Britain (exclusive of Ireland) amounted in

1801	. . .	to 10,942,000
1811	. . .	„ 12,609,000
1821	. . .	„ 14,391,000
1831	. . .	„ 16,537,000
And Ireland .		„ 8,000,000*

From 1700 to 1790 the increase in England and Wales was about 28 per cent.

From 1811 to 1821 . . . $17\frac{1}{4}$
„ 1821 to 1831 . . . 14

There were 10,000 females born to 10,435 males.

This increase of population is not in an inverse ratio with their physical well-being. On the con-

* Browning. 'Domestic and Financial Condition of Great Britain.'

trary, they are on the whole better fed, clothed, lodged, &c. than before. The fact is sufficiently proved by the vast decrease of mortality. This was

In 1740	.	.	.	.	1 in 35
1780	.	.	.	.	„ 40
1790	.	.	.	.	„ 45
1800	.	.	.	.	„ 47
1810	.	.	.	.	„ 53
1820	.	.	.	.	„ 59*

People in the country lived longer than those in towns, but the increase of population in the latter has far exceeded that in the former. In England, the men employed in agriculture are now 28 per cent.; in Ireland, 64 per cent.

	England.	Ireland.
In trade and manufactures,	42 per ct.	18 per ct.
Other employments	. . 30 „	18† „

The progress of medical science has tended to diminish the number of deaths. In the great hospital of St. Bartholomew they were,

In 1689	.	.	.	.	1 in 7
1740	.	.	.	.	„ 10
1780	.	.	.	.	„ 14
1813	.	.	.	.	„ 16
1827	.	.	.	.	„ 48

From 1780 to 1826 the yearly increase of the population was 180,000 souls; but that of the productive power, especially by means of machinery, 680,000, consequently the surplus produce was much greater. Three centuries ago,

* M'Culloch's Dictionary, p. 1141.
† 'Quarterly Review,' No. cv. p. 64.

perhaps 80 or 90 per cent. of the men were employed in husbandry, and did not create so large a surplus produce as the 28 per cent. do now.   While the increase of population has been, since 1780, about 90 per cent., the increase of agricultural production has been 86 per cent., and that of manufacturing and commercial production 400 per cent.   The population was,

In London and its	1831.	1832.	Increase per cent.
suburbs	1,225,000	1,471,000	20
Manchester	154,000	227,000	42
Glasgow	147,000	202,000	38
Liverpool	131,000	189,000	44
Edinburgh	138,000	162,000	18
Birmingham	106,000	142,000	33
Leeds	83,000	123,000	49
Bristol	87,000	103,000	19

The average increase of population in these cities was 25 per cent., but, for the whole of England, only 15 per cent.

These are very different facts from those presented by France,—with her exclusive preponderance of Paris.

I must break off for to-day, as both room and time are at an end.   Of the connected symptoms of vitality or of disease exhibited by England, another time.

The commentary on what I have reported to-day I may safely leave to yourself.

LETTER XXVII.

Municipal Reform Bill—Political Constitution of Villages—Report of Corporation Commission—Municipal Charters—Protest of Sir F. Palgrave—London Review—Radical scheme of Municipal Reform—Its resemblance to Municipal System of Prussia—Centralization—Royal Authority.

London, May 28th, 1835.

THE most important act of the last session of Parliament was the new Poor 'Law; the grand question in the present, will be the Church. Of these I have given you such an account as my time and powers permit.

The second great question which will come under debate, in the course of the present summer, relates to the Municipal institutions of England and Wales. I might do better to wait to see what will be said in Parliament. But perhaps you would rather learn, beforehand, something of the nature of the establishments of which such heavy complaints are heard here, and of which next to nothing is known in Germany.

I shall, therefore, first, give you the briefest possible sketch of the main points of the Report drawn up by the Parliamentary Commissioners, and supported by three folio volumes of evidence; secondly, notice the dissentient opinions expressed by Sir Francis Palgrave, partly in favour of the old institutions, and in opposition to that

of all the other Commissioners; thirdly, give you
some account of what the so-called radical party,
in their organ, the " London Review," requires;
and fourthly, add a few remarks relative to the
municipal institutions of Prussia.

First.—Among the corporations to which the
Commission referred, villages were not included,
though these are by no means without political
powers; either every parishioner has a voice in
the general vestry of the parish, or a " select
vestry," or committee, of from five to twenty persons, is chosen by that body. The latter mode
has often considerable advantages over the former;
for a small number of picked men are more
likely to inspect and administer affairs well, than
a large promiscuous body: the disadvantage,
however, was, that they were apt to degenerate
into party oligarchies, or, from indolence, to leave
the management in very few hands. Hence arose
disputes between the select vestry and the body
of the parishioners. Of late years, therefore, the
number of parishes whose affairs were under the
management of representatives has gradually
decreased *.

The worst, but the least frequent form, is that
in which the ruling body are not chosen by the
parish, but nominate their own members, and are
subject to no control or responsibility. In Oc-
tober, 1831, a bill was brought into Parliament †,
with a view to improve the system of representa-

* For the numbers here quoted by the author, see Report on the
Poor-Law, p. 117.—*Translator.*

† Hansard, viii. 822; ix. 767.

tion in rural parishes. One provision was, that the parishioners should have votes in proportion to their property,—the scale graduating from one to six. It was objected, that this would confer so enormous a preponderancy on wealth, that two or three persons would be able to domineer over all the others. Better to leave the old system, or to give one vote to every man paying taxes. The bill was thrown out on the 23rd of January, 1832.

The inquiries of the Commission embraced 246 corporations, which were in the possession and exercise of municipal rights, and (exclusive of London) comprised a population of 2,038,000 inhabitants. Some cities refused to furnish the information required, especially concerning their property and accounts; the greater number, however, facilitated the labours of the Commissioners in a laudable manner. It was less the object to inquire into their ancient constitutions, than to ascertain their present condition. The investigation, however, clearly proved that, in old times, cities were neither so democratically, nor so aristocratically, governed as many of the respective parties contended. Most of the existing charters were granted between the reign of Henry VIII. and the Revolution of 1668. The aim of almost all of them obviously was, to limit the rights of the people, and to make the ruling body independent of the citizens. Almost all are constructed on the principle of self-election. Charles II. and James II. more particularly endeavoured to effect such a change in all existing charters, that the whole power should pass into the hands of the crown, or of persons immediately dependent upon it. The Revolution of 1668 partially defeated this project; nevertheless all the charters granted down to the most recent times have been conceived in the same spirit, and show, as the Commission expresses itself, " a contempt of all systematic and consistent plan for the improvement of municipal institutions, or the adaptation of them to the advanced state of society."

The administrations of cities are now so extremely various and diffcrent, that it is hardly possible to discover any common feature by which to describe them. They may, however, be arranged under two main heads : those in which (either by charter or custom) the number of freemen or burgesses is definite, and those in which it is indefinite. Admission into the former is generally to be obtained only by nomination of the ruling body; and this is generally connected with certain conditions, though sometimes left entirely to caprice: partiality, presents, and bribes here naturally come into operation.

Admission to the indefinite bodies is obtained chiefly by birth or marriage, seldom by property. In both these classes, however, we find the distinction between freemen and mere inhabitants. In many cases a man cannot be admitted to the freedom of the city without first becoming a member of some guild, or company of a particular trade. In the city of London there are eighty-four of these. The privileges of the freemen consist chiefly in certain immunities from local taxes,

in claims to endowments, in local tribunals, &c.
They have seldom any share in the choice of their
magistrates, or the share is very limited. The
chief magistrate is the mayor, whose powers and
privileges are very various. Associated with him
is a council, which, in some towns, is divided into
aldermen and common-councilmen. The mayor
is generally chosen out of this body, the members
of which usually hold their places for life, and fill
all the vacancies which occur without the partici-
pation of the freemen, or of the other inhabitants.

The mayor and council conduct the whole
affairs of the city. The assessment of local taxes
or rates, the appointment and salaries of subordinate officers—in short, all patronage, rests with
them. They have also civil and criminal courts,
though with very different powers and regulations.

The financial condition of the cities differs very
widely. The revenues are far from being always
well administered: many are plunged in debt by
carelessness and extravagance. The manner of
keeping the accounts is liable to many objections;
they are seldom properly examined, and scarcely
ever submitted to the public. There is a general
disposition to keep the inhabitants in the dark.
The schools are neglected, and the endowments
for the maintenance of them, which exist in such
abundance in England, are seldom honestly applied. There are numerous other complaints of
administrative abuses or neglects; but, above all,
of the partial and improper interference at the
general elections. To answer certain ends, in some
places the freedom of the city is constantly re-

fused; while, in others, a great number of persons are admitted to take up their freedom just before an election, in order to secure a majority to the side favoured by the magistrates.

The proofs in support of these allegations of the Commissioners are contained, as I said, in three thick folios, from which I cannot attempt even to extract. It appears, however, that the notion was very prevalent, and generally acted upon, that the town property was given in trust to the ruling body, to be administered for their own exclusive benefit.

The gross revenue of all the cities subjected to investigation (exclusive of London) was

About . . . £366,000
The expenditure . . 377,000
The debts . . . 1,860,000

As the very important point, the admission to, and exclusion from, the rights of citizenship, cannot be made clear to you by mere words, nor, consequently, the advantages or defects be intelligible, I am obliged to have recourse to a few figures, which throw unexpected light on this dark, or at least very misty, region.

[Here follow lists, extracted from the Report of the Corporation Commission, of the number of freemen or burgesses in towns or cities, in which the franchise is ' indefinite,' and in those in which it is ' definite.' Also a list of the number of freemen, or burgesses, as compared with the population of certain towns and cities.]

In Ipswich, which contains 28,000 inhabitants, eleven-twelfths of the property of the town is excluded from the franchise; one fifty-fifth of the inhabitants are burgesses, and pay one-twentieth of the town rates ; of these privileged individuals, one-ninth are *paupers*. No wonder if, with such institutions, systematical bribery (to use the words of the Commission) has been organised at general elections. So much for the Report of the Commission.

Secondly.—I come now to the protest which Sir Francis Palgrave entered against this Report. He asserts, that the Commissioners have suffered themselves to be too much influenced by the opinions of the day, and have given to their work the form and colour of a general accusation, rather than of an historical statement, which ought to exhibit merits and defects with perfect impartiality. That the consequences deduced from the evidence often did not really follow from it, or a general conclusion or condemnation was drawn from two or three cases. Accidental and personal vices, he alleges, are not sufficiently distinguished from those inherent in the municipal institutions themselves ; or defects incident to the whole country (such as those in the administration of justice, in schools, &c.), are represented as belonging exclusively to those institutions. Some abuses might be remedied by a change of persons ; some, of local institutions ; some, of the laws of the realm : these different cases are not sufficiently distinguished, and a general alteration in the corporations is constantly suggested as the universal remedy. The Commissioners further assert that there are universal signs of mistrust, dissatisfaction, and hatred against the existing corporations, although there is no sufficient evidence of this, or the complaints had been declared to be unfounded. In some cases individuals are made answerable for things which are the inevitable result of circumstances ; in others, on the contrary, the existing institutions are condemned on account of the culpable behaviour of individuals. Sometimes the inconveniences of the present system have been diminished by the ability of the magistrates; and sometimes the corporate power has checked the faults of individuals. It is certainly a mistake (as the example of Plymouth proves) to think that a very numerous body of electors affords any security for good systematic government.

Notwithstanding these and other objections to the partiality of the representations, and crudeness of the views, of the Commissioners, Sir Francis Palgrave assented, in the main, both to their censures and their suggestions, only in a softened manner. For example: he confesses that many things in the corporations are antiquated and inapplicable; the gradual improvement and cultivation of the people neglected; many details of law and police susceptible of improvement: he even declares himself against close corporations, and in favour of the choice of magistrates by the citizens. But he would give the crown the right of control and interference, and make the necessary reforms spring, not so much from a general law, as from various distinct changes adapted to the several local circumstances.

In a former work, ' Observations on the Principles to be adopted in the establishment of new

Municipalities,' Sir Francis Palgrave remarks, with great justice, that many of the municipal institutions of the middle ages were not so absurd as the ignorant and one-sided partisans of the present, or rather the future, pretend; and that, to be understood, they should be viewed on both sides. In this work he gave a sketch of a municipal system, which, in many points, agrees with his present suggestions; in others, differs from them. A more thorough examination of it would lead me too far from my main object. I therefore turn to,

Thirdly, The first number of the new ' London,' or, as it is called, Radical ' Review.' The principles and the suggestions of the writer are, in the main, as follows:—The boundaries of the existing corporations are extremely arbitrary; the more ancient parts subject to different magistrates from the more modern; and the necessity for one central point, and for an organic connexion, often entirely overlooked. The degree of power, and the extent of jurisdiction, of the magistrates is not fixed according to any general principles; for instance—judicial authority is connected with it in one place, and not in another. It were much better to have courts of justice established in all towns, on a uniform footing; with an appeal to the courts of Westminster in the most important cases. This would obviate the expense, loss of time, &c., of attending the courts of session and assize, and the disadvantages of tribunals composed of persons so incompetent as the present magistrates and country gentlemen generally are.

Nor is the administrative branch of municipal government in a more satisfactory state than the judicial. Various measures, merely of local interest, such as lighting with gas, &c., must now be referred to Parliament, whence arise needless expense and delay to all parties. The judicial, administrative, and legislative functions ought to be severed. One judge is enough for each court, but he must be a lawyer, and not changed like the mayors. All ten-pound householders (or, still better, *all* householders) should be free of the city. The elections to be annual, and by ballot. Every civic functionary to have his allotted business. As they are all equal, the office of mayor is useless; they should choose a mayor from among their own body. The whole body of the burgesses to choose a certain number, as a legislative body; these should not act as judges, nor as administrators,—merely as law-makers. Every citizen to be eligible; for qualifications, especially pecuniary ones, have never been found to produce any good results on the choice of such legislative bodies. The financial officers to be changed yearly, and to exhibit their accounts on resigning their office. All members of the magistracy to have certain salaries: unpaid functionaries never acquit themselves of their duties properly.

Instead of entering into any detailed observations on the Prussian municipal system, or any comparison of its several provisions with what I have now told you, I shall content myself with one most important and conclusive fact; viz., that in

Prussia—thanks to the king's wise and beneficial reforms—all the grievances of which the
English now complain are redressed, and all the
improvements which they demand are introduced.

The conflict between the Old and the New will
certainly be very vehement; and the one party
will, as usual, want to retain, the other to alter,
too much.   A reform of the corporations is, however, so essentially connected with other reforms,
and is so greatly for the interest of the majority,
that it is impossible it should be much longer
postponed.

The monopoly of a few privileged persons must
give way to a wider right of citizenship; the self-
election of a small body of magistrates, to some
freer form of election by the citizens; and, above
all, some control must be established over the
management of the finances.

Our municipal system exhibits a safer and
better middle way than English Ultras imagine.

*   *   *   *   *

After these general remarks, you must indulge
me in a *quodlibet* of particular ones.

1st. I said something to you (in my letter on
the poor-laws) about the administration of villages.   I must add that there are no villages
(*Bauer-Gemeinen*), in our sense of the word, in
England.   More of this another time.

2nd. Many, indeed the most important, suggestions of the 'London Review' are in perfect
accordance with the actual institutions of Prussia.
There are others from which I must dissent.—For
instance, that one judge is sufficient for a local

court; that all functionaries should be changed yearly : that a mayor or bürgermeister is unnecessary, and that no qualification whatever is to be required from any of the legislative body. The possession of a house (if it be not mortgaged for its full value) is, in fact, a pecuniary qualification; and certain acquirements—a certain degree of education—might, perhaps, be more indispensable to a law-maker than that particular sum of money.

3rd. On the other hand, I cannot agree with Sir Francis Palgrave in making the right of citizenship dependent on length of residence in a town. Many a new settler who hires a house acquires a better claim than artisans and labourers who have lived there for years.

4th. We must never lose sight of the consideration that, in England, municipal are intimately connected with national rights; the elections for magistrates, with elections for members of parliament; and thus the political parties of a city have an importance of which we in Germany have scarcely a conception. For this very reason great care ought to be taken not to give a preponderancy to the democratical element; i. e. large popular assemblies. The monarchical element, represented by the mayor and council, the aristocratical, by the legislative body, should maintain their due weight if we would avoid confusion.

5th. This object cannot be attained by one sweeping law, which overlooks all local and individual considerations. A city like London, and cities which are almost in the category of rotten boroughs, require a very different organization; and it is an improvement in the new edition of our Prussian municipal code, that it pays more attention than the former to the concrete, and to existing differences.

6th. It is certainly a gross anomaly, that the number of the national electors is now much larger than the number of the town electors, or burgesses. This circumstance alone would suffice to make it impossible, after the passing of the Reform Bill, to adhere to the old system of close corporations, and to exclude the most respectable, instructed, and wealthy inhabitants of a city, legally, or rather arbitrarily, from the rights of citizenship.

7th. These rights, it is objected, are private rights, with which it is not the province of the general legislature to interfere. Independent of the arguments which have already been opposed to this great and fundamental error, I must observe that this assumed inviolability of corporations is not supported even by history; and, moreover, that if this principle be consistently followed out, the State would be resolved, or rather split up, into a number of independent parts. Without supreme control, these would almost necessarily fall into the hands of small oligarchical tyrannies; or, in case the new legislature went into the opposite extreme, the consequence would be democratical anarchy. We complain, and sometimes with reason, of being governed too much; but here are evident marks of being governed too little. If you say this, you are answered on every side, ' We govern ourselves; we do not want to be guided and governed as you inexperienced, immature people do.'

But I would just ask,—after what fashion the poor, the church, the schools, have governed themselves ? and what sort of organization is that which the close towns and boroughs have constructed for themselves? That enlargement of citizenship and civic rights,—that extension of the democratic element, which is carried further in Prussia than it ever was in Athens or Florence, or any state antient or modern,—can be productive of security and prosperity only when an administration composed of men rigorously examined, carefully chosen, and tranquil in the continued exercise of their functions presides over it ; when all individualities are united in one whole; and, lastly, when the necessity of a general supreme control is recognised by the people.

There is certainly such a thing as an oppressive, vexatious centralization, which crushes all political life and energy in the provincial population and authorities, and this exists in France. But there is also a want of centralization, which leads to the greatest discrepancies, inequalities, and contradictions; such as were here displayed in the management of the poor, but which, since this branch of the public service has been put under the control of national functionaries, are no longer possible. Since the passing of the Reform Bill, the superior power of the Lower House and the daily control exercised by the press and by public opinion, render it absurd and silly to talk of the danger of a ministerial tyranny or a bureaucracy.

The new organization of the towns and of the rural districts seems to require some change in the functions and competency of the Ministry of the Home Department: if some influence were conceded to the crown in this department, it would perhaps be for the good of the whole, and would serve to restore that balance of power which may otherwise, unhappily for England, be lost. It is not by rotten boroughs, by the capricious nomination or dismissal of ministers, by sinecures, secular or ecclesiastical, by attempts to strengthen the power of the peers, that the regal authority can in future make itself respected :—all these expedients are worn out and dead. I see no other possible way of giving it vigour and stability than in the direction I have pointed out. At all events, instructed and sagacious men will be more likely to come into these views, than into the ultra-Tory opinions which the Berlin ' Wochenblatt,' in its proclamation against Peel, enounces as the quintessence of true wisdom.

LETTER XXVIII.

Party at Lord ——'s—Pictures—English Society—Vacuity of
‘Routs’ — Ballot — Sir Robert Peel — Dissenters — Duke of
Wellington and Oxford—Shades of Toryism—English and
German Universities — Lord Brougham — Foreign popular
Education—Study of History in England—Duke of S.—
King's Birth-day Processions—Mail Coaches—Party at Lord
L——'s — Statues — Dresses — Aristocratical Blood and
Beauty—London ‘ Squeezes ’—Dinners—Judges in 'West-
minster Hall—Tieck—Stepney Papers—Mr. Faraday—Royal
Institution.

London, May 23, 1835.

At ten o'clock at night I was heartily tired, and
should gladly have gone to bed; but I wiped the
sleep out of my eyes, dressed myself in my best,
and drove to Lord ——'s. His wealth is obvious at
the very entrance of his house, and no less so the
tasteful employment of it. The magnificent staircase is decorated with works of art, and the saloons
filled with pictures of such merit, that his gallery
may, perhaps, be esteemed the first in England.
Three Raphaels, two exquisite Claudes, several of
the finest Titians;—here is matter for a long dis-
quisition. But this is Waagen's privilege—or
rather his duty; and I shall be able to refresh
my own recollections by his description. I proved
my connoisseurship by attributing to Domeni-
chino (on certain grounds which I cannot detail
here) a forest with nymphs, hitherto ascribed to
Annibal Caracci. Waagen had already expressed
the same opinion to the possessor.

Lord —— received me with courteous expressions, but in the crowd of distinguished persons
who kept arriving could not, of course, trouble
himself any further about me.   An elegant and
beautiful woman was so compassionate as to
enter into conversation with me on some literary
subjects, and on recollections of Italy.   She remarked that there were too few people for such
large rooms; that one could not move about
freely.   Did she mean that there was no freedom till the mass put an end to the stiffness,
and made curious critical observation impossible ?

That, in companies of this kind, the host and
hostess can pay no attention to any individual, is
evident enough: but the unintelligible names
which are shouted into the room by servants as
the guests throng in, are superfluous to those
who know them, and not of the least use to those
who know them not.   An Englishman would be
greatly astonished, not to say alarmed, if I were
to presume upon this proclamation of his name to
address him as an acquaintance.   It never occurs
to any body to make this a ground of speaking
to a stranger.

These 'routs,' therefore, can have no other
interest for a foreigner than that of a *spectacle;*
as soon as the first impression is over they are
perfectly barren.   He can get at no conversation
in which there is the least instruction, amusement
or excitement.   Even those who know each other
flit up and down, like the atoms of Epicurus,
without combining into any form, or seeming to

have any centre or any object. Some may say this mobility is a proof of a high state of civilization; and that a German or a Dutchman, who remains immoveably attached to the same seat for hours and hours, with his pipe in his mouth, is not a very amusing companion.

But there is an agreeable interval between these two extremes. A well-bred German host does not give his attention for a whole evening to any individual guest, but, if he has once accepted him as a good bill, he does not lay him aside, but endorses him to some other person in the company, he to a third, and so on; and this sort of currency, this *giro,* is agreeable to all, and burthensome to none.

I send you such a quantity of politics, and in such masses, that you may see in what way I am likely to regard and interpret the various newspaper reports. I don't want therefore to send you the small wares of daily comments; and yet things often occur which I wish to communicate. To-day you must accept some of these trifles.

Lord John Russell's defeat in Devonshire has turned the public attention strongly to the ballot. It is warmly discussed in letters and articles of all sorts, and all its merits and defects thoroughly brought to light. This is one great advantage of England: would our censorship allow another newspaper to attempt a confutation of the ' Wochenblatt,' in order that truth might come out more clearly from this double trial?

Secondly, Peel's ministerial defence of an untenable fortress displayed more ability than the beginning of his opposition campaign, in which he reproached ministers with not proposing reforms or changes enough for this session. He appeared as advocate of the Dissenters, whose adversary he had been for years, and, on the subject of the Marriage Bill, adopted and urged thoroughly Whig principles; just as he formerly did with regard to Catholic Emancipation. The result was, that all the Dissenting Members of the House declared that they were quite willing to wait, under the present Ministry; and that Mr. Spring Rice defeated this insidious attack with the simplest arguments.

Thirdly.—Wellington, who is more of an old Tory than Peel, and, as such, is the steadfast defender of Oxford against all attacks, however just and obvious, lately recommended to the Heads of Houses, and all who have a voice in the matter, to cease to make a subscription to thirty-nine intricate and dogmatical articles of faith the condition of the admission of young men to college. He proposed to substitute a rational declaration, fully adequate to the protection of the church and religion; and thus, on one point at least, to comply with the wishes of the country. His proposal has, however, been rejected by 459 votes to 57. A singular sign of the times! a proof that reform, progressive reform, appears necessary even to those who long beheld, or tried to behold, in the actually existing the eternally perfect. What gradations in Toryism, from the Duke of Cumberland to Peel and Stanley! They are as far from being all of a mind as their opponents. Far from considering this a reproach to them, I am delighted to see that a few abstractions are not sufficient to bind together a number of men like a bundle of sticks; that their intellectual individualities predominate over the affinity of their pursuits and interests. This diversity shows a richer organization, both individual and national.

As (by way of fulfilling Holberg's prophecy of the eternal existence of the electoral princes) the Elector of Hesse held fast to his title, although there was nothing more to elect,—so Oxford will represent the immobility of high Toryism, *in perpetuam rei memoriam.* But the earth turns, and will turn, however stubbornly we may deny that it moves; nay, not only the earth and the planets, but even suns and fixed stars, are borne along in this dance; and Oxford, though she may pout and turn her back on the rest of the world, will be forced to make the *dos-à-dos* with them, in her own despite. Remarkable, that the English universities always drag behind, while the German are accused of striding before on stilts! This accusation may be well founded as to some; but most of the German universities have idols of their own, before which they fall down, and which it is held to be the duty of every well-intentioned professor to worship.

Fourthly.—Lord Brougham, in proposing some measures for the improvement of the education of the people, which is now in so defective a state, took occasion to say that, on the continent, it was forbidden to teach " civil history" in the popular schools; and then went into a grand panegyric on the study of history, and a philippic against the tyranny of foreign governments. I will not ask, like the Greek on hearing the eulogium on Hercules, " Who blamed him ?" but one has a right to ask *where* the study of history is prohibited, and from what sources Lord Brougham derived the materials for his praise and for his censure ? At least, he needed not have made all Europe the object of his attack. He should not shoot into the air, but should point more accurately to those whom he, as " far-reaching Apollo," intended to hit. I can't help thinking that there is some mistake of the reporter, or the printer, at the bottom of this. Lord Brougham urged the necessity of an improvement in the English establishments for education, and cited as one of their most striking defects, that neither at Eton, nor at Oxford, neither at King's College, nor at the London University—the child of his fancy or his wisdom—in short, that nowhere was history properly taught: for that professors who were to be, or might be, appointed, could not be reckoned; any more than professors who gave lectures which nobody attended. And least of all does Lord Brougham's panegyric apply to the fragments about Assyrians and Babylonians, or the miserable bald outlines of Greek and Roman history, which are appended here and there to philological exercises in England. Let us hope that Lord Brougham's eloquence will soon conjure into existence in this country, what Germany has so long possessed in such fullness and perfection.

Although I had gone to bed so late, I was at my writing-table again at seven in the morning, and worked till eleven, when I drove to Kensington to see the Duke of S——. I found him alone, in his dressing gown; and as he began the conversation in German, I naturally continued it in the same language. Thus it lasted for two hours, without a minute's interruption, without those capricious transitions from one subject to another which so often occur, and without descending to insignificant topics. It turned chiefly upon England and her political affairs, or on matters of universal interest. The Duke spoke, of course, like a Whig, and lamented the want not only of just views on the events and circumstances of the times, but even of a knowledge of constitutional law.

From Kensington I walked through the shady gardens to Hyde-park corner, and then turned from the Green-park to St. James's park and St. James's palace. I arrived at half-past two, just in time to see the carriages drive up, in honour of William IV.'s birth-day. If 1800 persons, exclusive of those attached to the court, walked past the king in gala dresses that day, certainly there were 900 carriages in motion; for, on an average, there were not more than two persons in each. The horses and carriages were brilliant; the servants in all colours, laced and covered with ribands and fringe. They wore breeches and white silk stockings; the footmen had large cocked hats, like those of our military officers, and the coachmen little three-cornered hats, under which peeped forth a bobwig. Inside the carriáges, too, were wigs of all dimensions; but these attracted my attention less than the women, who appeared in the full splendour of nature and of art. As the procession moved on very slowly, and was obliged to make a halt at every tenth step, I took the liberty of moving on in a parallel line, and of keeping by the side of certain carriages which contained the greatest beauties. There is no opportunity, no company, in the world in which one may stare ladies in the face with so much ease—I might almost say impudence—and for so long a time. This *revue spéciale, unique* in its kind, is a far nobler and more beautiful sight than a *revue spéciale* of soldiers. I tried to figure to myself all their circumstances, and to read the thoughts of each in her eyes. The persons in the first carriage, who were afraid of being the first, had anxieties of quite a different nature from those of the tall blonde who closed the procession. Which equipage was the most beautiful?—which the least so?—which dress was the richest or the most elegant?—which was the queen of the fair and sumptuous train? An unfortunate hackney coach, with a dirty coachman, and a still more beggarly footboy, had got among these brilliant equipages. Those who were within, whether they were presentables or not, had drawn up the wooden blinds so high that one could not see them. They must have been very uncomfortable, and I was glad

that I was on my own legs, in freedom, and not
in their place.

When this was all over I went and read at the
Athenæum. Just as I was preparing to go
away, Mr. M——, the secretary of the club, who
makes it his business to oblige every one in every
possible manner, called me back, and told me that
if I would wait till six o'clock, I should see something which London alone could show. I was
least of all in a humour to doubt that to-day; for
as I had seen in the Duke of S—— a royal prince,
and in the train of equipages, an aristocracy, such
as exist in no other country in the world, it was
now the turn for the democracy   From the bal-
cony of the Athenæum, at the corner of Pall Mall
and Waterloo-place, perhaps the handsomest
part of London, I saw crowds of people, horsemen
and carriages of all sorts; troops of children, with
flowers and flags, incessantly shouting ' God save
the King !' and so forth. But it was not only
this that Mr. M—— had invited me to see : it was
more particularly the procession of all the London
mail coaches; for they also had been to give their
huzza to the king, and passed by here on their
return. At last the long-expected train arrived ;—
the coachman sitting on the box, the guard
behind outside, both dressed in new suits of scarlet, and ornamented with flowers and ribands.
Inside the brightly-varnished coaches sat their
wives, daughters, or friends—a parody on the
fashionable ladies. I was too far off to institute
a comparison between the aristocracy and the
democracy; but the superb horses and the excel-

XXVIII.]   KING'S BIRTHDAY.   53

lent harness made a great impression on me.
Such a splendid display of carriages-and-four as
these mail-coaches and their horses afforded could
not be found, or got together, in all Berlin.   It
was a real pleasure to see them in all the pride
and strength which half an hour later was to send
them in every direction with incredible rapidity, to
every corner of England.   The improvements in
our administration of the post are certainly very
great, and in many respects our coaches are more
convenient than these; but, compared with the
countless host of these magnificent horses, the
German ones are miserable Rosinantes.

I then hastened to Mr. ——, to deliver my
ponderous letter on the Reform Bill, and, to my
great delight, found yours, which I answered on
a separate sheet of paper; dined at eight; hastened home; dressed for a second time, and then
went out to look at the illuminations in a few of
the streets.   The usual device was ' W. R. and a
Crown,' and only a few about St. James's-street
and Waterloo-place were rendered splendid and
beautiful by coloured lamps and moving gas-
lights; the greater number of houses and streets
remained unilluminated; nevertheless the crowd
was enormous, and, in some places, indeed dangerous; so that I thanked God when I got away
from the bright spots into darkness.

When I went to the Marquis of L——'s, at
half-past eleven, there were but few people in the
spacious and beautiful rooms, so that I was able
to enjoy undisturbed the delight of looking at the
remarkably fine statues.   They were admirably

lighted from above, and had a beautiful effect
against the red velvet background of the niches.
The gallery and drawing-rooms filled gradually,
and I was enabled to continue my observations
of the morning. The gentlemen were, to-day,
chiefly in scarlet uniforms; some were in em-
broidered court dresses, with bagwigs fastened to
the collar of the coat. The ladies were more
attractive than the gentlemen; they were generally dressed in white silk, or in other materials
of the finest kind and of that colour. Only two or
three older ones had hats or other head-dresses; a
very few had caps, if so one may call such light
transparent head-dresses. White satin shoes,
stockings, so thin or so coloured that the feet appeared naked. None *coiffées à la Chinoise*, but with
the forehead uncovered, and long ringlets hang-.
ing down to the neck; some with shorter curls, or
with the hair braided. At the back of the head
were edifices of hair of various kinds, and in
these the feathers were fastened. Five or six
of the youngest of the ladies had nothing on
the head; the others, old and young, wore a
number of white ostrich feathers, fastened in the
manner I have described. Here and there, as an
exception, was seen a blue, red, or yellow feather:
in front was a diadem, a flower, or an ornament
of the most sparkling brilliants.

If the House of Lords becomes, as it is feared
it will, unpopular, or is menaced by any dangers,
the wisest thing their Lordships could do would
be to retreat into the rear, and to station their
beautiful wives and daughters in front to defend

them: nobody could resist them; they would carry all before them.   An aristocracy of such blood as this is certainly not physically *usée*.   Almost all that the highest circles of London can offer (with the exception of some ultra Tories) was assembled at the Marquis of L——'s; but

" Wer nennet ihren Namen ? Wer ?"

My desire of making acquaintances in company is natural, and I was accordingly introduced to a few persons; but such a wish only proved that I knew nothing of English routs, and that I asked something quite impossible and absurd.   When I had come to the conviction . that these assemblies had as little the purpose of conversation as of eating and drinking, I had made one step towards knowledge; and I then imagined that the object was to look and be looked at; but I had not yet hit the mark; for yesterday evening people placed themselves so that one could not even see.   At a German supper sometimes one guest more comes than the table can conveniently hold, and the party sit somewhat crowded : in a Paris *soirée*, twenty or thirty more arrive than there are chairs for ; but here, more people meet together than can find standing-room.   Indeed one was more crowded than in the street, only that the company did not move about so rapidly, but stood nearly still, whereas the populace have a peculiar pleasure in the act of pushing and elbowing.   It took me a full half hour to make my way from the farthest room to the entrance; it was utterly impos-

sible to press through faster. As I went out,
guests were still arriving, and the number of the
carriages in waiting was so great that the ladies
went out and traversed the spacious court on
foot, that they might reach them sooner. I went
to bed at two o'clock, after this long, gay day.

Saturday, May 30th.

I hope you will not blame me if I sometimes
contradict my own reports, and send you correc-
tions of what I have told you before. Day unto
day showeth knowledge; but if, for that reason, I
would wait for the last day in England before I
wrote anything, I must wait till I got home, and
leave you all the while without tidings. What
would be gained, perhaps, in objective truth,
would be more than lost in directness and vivid-
ness of the impressions. This naturally finds
utterance first, and according to personal character, habits of thinking and feeling; but then
come doubts; and with me, more especially, the
endeavour to place myself exactly in the situation
of others (as it beseems a ' *historiker*,' above all
men). Sometimes, however, one can get no further than the knowledge that a thing exists; or
that such a thing is just so, and no otherwise:
one cannot acquire any taste for it, or find oneself
at all at ease in one's new position.

This is my case with the London ' routs,' or,
as they are more expressively called, ' squeezes.'
—In both names, however, the English seem
to express ridicule or censure of themselves;

and a foreigner may, therefore, be more pardonable if he ventures to doubt of the excellence of this form of social intercourse. That all that Germans understand by, or require from, society, is totally inapplicable to these parties, I have already admitted. In this world of necessity, it signifies nothing that a person moves about as one atom among countless other atoms— should speak, see, hear,—or not, as he can; he must take the thing as it is—as something predestinate, and please himself with it as he best can. This, then, I most honestly do: I rejoice in my invitations, and in my experiences, and in things new and unheard of in Germany. Yet, I must confess, the doubt *will* return, whether among the various and refined forms of human society, such ' squeezes' merit a place; and whether they ought not rather to be reckoned monstrous— abnormal? The Germans sometimes lose themselves in the same region with their great feasts, and the English have certainly the advantage, that, with a saving of the food, and of various inconveniences, *they* accomplish as much:—that is to say, the German may reply, nothing; while, at least, we eat and drink well, and can generally talk at our ease to our next neighbour without elbowing and crowding.

*   *   *   *   *   *   *

Yesterday I dined with a small party, at the house of a son of Mr. T——. I sat near the hostess, an agreeable woman, and a physician, who had studied in Germany, and spoke very good German. I had determined to go home early; but I fell into such a long conversation with an uncle of Mr. T——, on agriculture, leases, &c., on which he gave me much information, that midnight arrived before I was aware.

In the morning I saw the Judges of England, in Westminster Hall, in their red gowns and long wigs, and opposite to them the black advocates, with their curled wigs. As there was no criminal trial going on, but only a civil action, I went away very shortly.

I declined going to see hospitals, because they are not in my province, and my time is so extremely limited.

Sunday, May 1st.

My first thoughts and wishes to-day were devoted to Tieck. May Heaven long preserve him, to pour forth upon the world the treasures of his fancy and his genius! He must ever be the delight of all who have the intellect and the sensibility requisite to understand and to feel his exquisite graces. Hereafter it will hardly be believed that men have existed who could eagerly drink down the nauseous draught of modern French literature, concocted of every foul and disgusting ingredient, and turn away coldly or contemptuously from this Hippocrene, which flowed in golden purity and silver sweetness by their side. But it would be unjust to leave this judgment to posterity alone; we will bear witness that there existed in Germany a public capable of understanding and feeling the beauty, the nobleness, the symmetry, the profound feeling, and the gay humour which are the characteristics of Tieck.

After this out-pouring of love and anger, I turn to the history of yesterday.   My conscience drove me to the Museum, and I had five large volumes of the famous Stepney papers laid before me. Stepney was messenger to several Courts, and this collection treats of the latter years of the seventeenth, and the beginning of the eighteenth century.   Two of these volumes contain letters of Lord Raby from Berlin, and though I did not expect any important political facts, I thought I should find amusing matter respecting manners, customs, &c., but I was disappointed.   There was a great deal indeed about hunting, fishing, weddings, funerals, quarrels for precedence, distributions of orders, &c.; but when these things are described neither with psychological acuteness, nor with wit and pleasantry, nor with reference to their deeper and more serious bearings, they soon lose all significance and interest, and history has not the slightest concern with them.

I therefore lost patience, and went away before three o'clock to hear Mr. Faraday, the celebrated chemist, lecture on zinc.   As I know nothing of chemistry, and never could discover in myself the least talent for it, I contented myself with the knowledge I had; viz., that the residence of the true Prince of Zinc is in Silesia, where he weighs and counts his treasure, and will some time or other be raised to as high a station among the metallic demi-gods, as his predecessor and cousin Rübezahl enjoys among the botanical ones. This fundamental part of the science of zinc and zincdom, Mr. Faraday seemed entirely ignorant of.

He spoke only of zinc presses, zinc pendulums, the affinity between zinc and copper; in short, of matters which the Zinc Prince, who surely ought to know best, says nothing about.

To be serious, the lecture was highly interesting even to the ignorant and uninitiated. Mr. Faraday is not only a man of profound chemical and physical science, (which all Europe knows,) but a very remarkable lecturer. He speaks with ease and freedom, but not with a gossiping, unequal tone, alternately inaudible and bawling, as some very learned professors do; he delivers himself with clearness, precision, and ability. Moreover, he speaks his language in a manner which confirmed me in a secret suspicion I had, that a great number of Englishmen speak it very badly. Why is it that French in the mouth of Mdlle. Mars, German in that of Tieck, English in that of Faraday, seems a totally different language?—because they articulate, what other people swallow or chew. It is a shame that the power and harmony of simple speech, (I am not now talking of eloquence but of vowels and consonants,) that the tones and inflexions which God has given to the human voice, should be so neglected and abused. And those who think they do them full justice,—preachers,—generally give us only the long straw of pretended connoisseurs, instead of the chopped straw of the dilettanti.

The large room at the Royal Institution, Albemarle Street, where Mr. Faraday lectured, is a semicircle, or rather a $\frac{3}{4}$ circle, lined with benches and galleries to the very roof. Of the three or four hundred hearers, at least half were women.

After the lecture a gentleman exhibited the model of a steam-engine half a finger long, and of the power, not of many horses, nor even half horses, but of half a flea; and the little monster moved with as much rapidity and regularity as those enormous sea-dragons which force their way against the elements.

LETTER XXIX.

Codification—Ignorance of Roman Law in England—Notion of the
absolute perfection of English Law exploded—Lord Brougham's
Speech—Anomalies—Rejection of Bills by the Lords—Law of
Inheritance—Centralization of Justice—Quarterly and Edinburgh Reviews—Practical Men—Local Courts' Bill—Debate—
Prussian Law—Influence and Interests of Lawyers—House
of Lords—Vocation of an Aristocracy—Registration.

London, May 28th, 1835.

THE German jurists who are opposed to codification are certainly right, if it is meant that these
codes are to consist entirely of new inventions;
that every thing heretofore existing is to be abolished, and the thread of history thus completely
snapped. But they are wrong if their veneration
is directed towards the *moles indigesta* under
which the camels of the law set so many useless
steps in their juristical treadmill. At all events,
what is scattered may be collected; what is obso-
lete, laid aside; what is still available, arranged
in its proper place; and, appended to the esoteric
science, (often mere drudgery and pedantry,)
some exoteric instruction in law and jurisprudence
be prepared, and made intelligible to the people.
In these respects the Prussian '*Landrecht*' is certainly an advance upon the Roman law books.
Least of all should Romanists appeal to the
example or the authority of England, where
hardly any thing is known of systematic Roman

law; while, at the same time, there is such an
entire absence of any such thing as an English
code of any collection or manual of the laws of
England actually in force, that the universal
answer to all my inquiries is, that a foreigner
never will, or can, arrive at a single clear idea
about it. I must therefore.venture, from the
depths of my ignorance, to report a few of the
most recent juristical events.

The assertion so long and so intrepidly made,
that the English administration of justice could
not be improved; that it had attained absolute
perfection, and that every alteration must necessarily be for the worse, has, together with a
number of similar maxims about the constitution
of parliament, the necessity of sinecures, the protection of native industry, and so on, been, if
not theoretically, yet practically, given up. Here
and there only a solitary citadel is defended by
the immovables. Romilly, Peel, Brougham,—men
of the most different characters,—have equally
put their hand to the work of improvement, and
have already effected many beneficial changes.
Many no less desirable have been vehemently and
successfully opposed. I shall give some examples
of this.

Lord Brougham's speech of the 7th Jan. 1828,
on the state of the legislation, (I don't mean to
go further back,) touches on a great number of
the defective points. I can only glance over
a few detached ones.

We have, says he, in London, three high courts
of justice, the jurisdiction of which is nearly the

same. Whilst, however, their functions are substantially the same, there are great and capricious differences in the procedure, the forms, costs, &c.; and while, for example, the Court of King's Bench is overloaded with business, the Court of Common Pleas and the Exchequer have little to do—partly because, in these, a few barristers enjoy a mischievous monopoly. The judges have little prospect of advancement : they are apt to become mere pedantic and technical lawyers, from the monotonous routine in which they move ; and as their number has not been increased, with the vast increase of business, delay and precipitation are inevitable.

The Privy Council exercises the supreme jurisdiction over the colonies, for which it forms a very unsuitable and inconvenient tribunal. The expense, the distance, the delay, are sufficient to deter parties from resorting to it : so that, in fact, the obstacles amount to a denial of justice. Add to this, the inconveniences arising from the variety of laws prevailing in the colonies—Dutch, French, Danish, Spanish, Mohammedan, Indian— of the greater part of which the Privy Council are necessarily ignorant.

Nor is the boasted institution of Justices of the Peace less open to objection. Their appointment is exclusively in the hands of Lords-Lieutenant of counties ; and their enormous power is subject to no supervision or control whatever.

The laws which regulate real property, inheritance, and other important matters, without any sufficient reason, differ very much in different

parts of England. There is an unjust diversity
of forms for the treasury, and for private persons;
and the costs in many cases are so high, that a
man is severely punished by gaining his cause.
The costs of one suit in the Court of Chancery
were from seven to eight thousand pounds.*
And as trials may be protracted in various ways,
one favourable decision by no means puts an end
to litigation. An action for debt does not extend
to real property: nay, even the greater part of
personal property (*e. g.* bank-notes, public bonds,
&c.) are not liable to execution or seizure. Bankrupts only are compelled to make a distribution
of their effects; all other debtors, and their heirs,
may pay one creditor to the exclusion of the
others.

I might here adduce a whole list of the strangest
anomalies in the English law, which can be defended neither on philosophical nor historical
grounds; but I shall content myself with two
observations, confirmatory of the last-mentioned
subject of complaint, which I extract from the
parliamentary debates :—

Whatever (says one speaker†) be the amount
of real property which a man leaves at his death,
his creditors will not receive a farthing (except
from the good pleasure and honour of the heirs),
unless he leaves personal property also. If a
man borrows a sum of money, and immediately
devotes it to the cultivation of his land, the creditor, according to the existing law, has no redress

* Hansard, ii. 828.　　　† Hansard, xvii. 370.

whatsoever, if the debtor dies before a court of justice has adjudged the payment of the debt.

The bills which were prepared with a view to reform laws of such flagrant injustice were four times thrown out by the Lords. It is evident, that political considerations concerning the law of inheritance here exercised a sinister influence, and induced Noble Lords to justify, or at any rate to tolerate, acts of dishonesty and fraud in private transactions*.

As the English law of inheritance differs in so many respects from ours, I will endeavour to compress its leading principles for your information. They have, perhaps, more than any other cause whatsoever, contributed to make England what it is; and an alteration in them would probably have a more universal and pervading effect than the reform of the House of Commons.

All inheritances are divided into ' real property,' and 'personal property.' Both are, by law, at the absolute disposal of the father, except where the former is bound by a certain family settlement called an ' entail.' If he makes no disposition, the real property descends in a right line. Till within two years, relations in the ascending line could not inherit. Male descendants have precedence of females; and these, of collateral relations. Where there are several sons, the eldest inherits the whole real estate; and this applies not to the peerage alone. When there are no sons, daughters inherit

* Hansaid, xviii. 105.

equally. Collateral relations must be 'of the whole blood:' that is to say, the collateral heir, in whatever generation in the ascending line, must descend from the same father and the same mother. Half brothers and sisters, and all other persons related by the half blood, are excluded; or the most remote relation of the whole blood excludes the nearest of the half blood: *e. g.*, when a man has three daughters by the first wife, and one by the second, they inherit equally from their father; but if two daughters of the first marriage die without issue, the third takes the whole property of the two deceased sisters;—the fourth, nothing. Or, if a father has two sons by different mothers, and the eldest, who was his heir, dies without issue, the half-brother has no claim whatever to the property. Among collateral relations, those of the male line have always precedence over those of the female. According to the old common law, the personal estate is divided into three equal parts,— of which a third devolves to the descendants, a third to the widow, and a third might be disposed of by the possessor at his pleasure. If he had only children, or only a wife, either of these parties inherited the half, and the other half remained at his disposal: these portions were called, *rationabiles partes bonorum.* These provisions gradually underwent various changes, till, in the time of George the First, a law was passed, enacting that every man might leave his personalty or chattels at his own pleasure; and that neither his wife nor children should have any claim upon it against the dispositions of his will. If, therefore, the real property, *ab intestato, must* go to the eldest son, and the testator may bequeath all his other property to whom he will, it is clear that daughters and younger sons are worse provided for *by law* than in any other country; and that the aristocratical or oligarchical principles of England are at an immense distance from the more democratical or equalising institutions of other nations. And to this cause, I repeat, we may trace a great number of the most important phenomena: including that of the science of husband-catching, which I described in another letter. Only one question remains to be answered—How is the inheritance divided when the father has not made those testamentary provisions which the law allows? In that case, the widow takes a third, and the children, or their descendants, *per stirpes,* the remainder; or, in default of children and their issue, the widow takes a half, and the nearest relatives the other half. If there is no widow, the children take the whole; if there are neither, the property goes to the nearest relations, or their representatives; but no representation extends farther than to the children of brothers and sisters. I pass over many more detailed and remarkable provisions, because I am afraid of tiring you with these dry, though important, affairs.

London, May 29, 1835.

In my last letter I fell, I hardly know how, upon the law of inheritance; whereas my intention really was to touch upon another subject, which

affords matter of the greatest encomium and
exultation to one party, while the other represents
it as fraught with innumerable evils.

It will be difficult for a Prussian to believe that
there are no provincial or local tribunals, exer-
cising jurisdiction over matters of importance.
While everything that refers to, or depends on, one
general central point, every kind of centralization
is esteemed in this country a tyrannical invasion of
individual liberty; the centralization of the administration of justice in the capital (or at least in
the persons of the judges of the capital) is, with
singular inconsistency, carried to a pitch that ex-
ceeds every thing of which any other country can
furnish an example.   These metropolitan judges
travel about the country and give judgment, from
six months to six months, on an infinite number
and variety of things, in a few days.

Independently of this part of their functions,
the yearly number of the causes instituted in the
supreme courts of Westminster exceeded, in the
year 1827, eighty thousand.   Since that time
they have considerably increased.

While the ' Quarterly Review*' deplores these
and other defects and difficulties of procedure,
expense, &c., its opponent, the ' Edinburgh,' on
this occasion joining with it, exclaims, ' From the
want of local courts, and from a thousand other
devices and abuses, which have insinuated themselves into the law, the English have now the
worst administration of justice that can be found

* Vol. xlii. 183.

in any country !' And, together with this mischievous centralization, there exist numberless
arbitrary differences ; for instance, above two
hundred and forty courts for the recovery of
small debts ; scarcely two of which are governed
by the same principles. But the so-called ' practical men' acquire such a bigoted partiality for
their own class and their own narrow range of
technical learning, that they see in the removal of
absurdities nothing but mad and capricious inno-
vation.   Hence it was that Lord Brougham's
plan for local courts was defeated. He brought
it before the House of Lords in June, 1833 : the
following were some of the arguments he used in
its favour.*

The costs of proceedings in the courts of Westminster are so great, that they amount, in many
cases, to a denial of justice. Hence, many people
bring an action for a debt of 1*l.* 19*s.* 11*d.*, when
the real sum owed is 5*l.*, in order to reduce the
costs one-half. Very often people have actually
paid a demand for which there was not the slightest ground, rather than run the risk of an action
which, *even if they were successful*, would certainly
have cost them more than the amount of the unjust demand.   Further, as there is no tribunal at
hand, almost all actions or plaints must wait six
or eight months, till the travelling judges arrive
in the country.   Hence (not to mention other evil
consequences to suitors), it often happens, that
·the possibility of establishing the justice of their

* Hansard, xviii. 858.

case is entirely lost. On one day, in Lancaster, the aggregate value of fifty actions did not amount to 50*l.*, and all these trifling matters had been compelled to wait till the judges of the high courts of Westminster arrived to decide them.

For these and other reasons, it was thought expedient that local courts should be established, with authority to decide actions of debt to the amount of 100*l.*, and actions of other kinds to the amount of 50*l.* It should be left to the parties to agree whether or not a jury should be summoued. Questions of real property, tithes, &c., should still be decided by the superior courts.

[Here follow the objections contained in the speeches of Lords Lyndhurst and Wharncliffe, and the reply of Lord Brougham. See Hansard, xix. 308; xviii. 335.]

The bill was thrown out in the House of Lords on the 9th of July, 1833, by 73 votes to 68; since which time everything has gone on in the old way*. To this historical text I must append a few remarks.

Notwithstanding this excessive centralization of the administration of justice in England, the laws, forms, costs, &c., are by no means brought into any kind of uniformity; and here, as in Germany, champions are found for the most capricious and irrational diversities. The example of Prussia is, however, sufficient to prove that district courts, subject to a common court of appeal, are sufficient for the maintenance of a uniform system; if, indeed, the legislators are competent

---

* Hansard, xix. 371.

to the conception and expression of such a system. At least it would never occur to any body to introduce the advantages of centralization by the abolition of all local tribunals.

Unquestionably, an intimate acquaintance with parties and circumstances may occasionally lead local judges into partiality; but still oftener (if they are men of any integrity at all) this accurate knowledge of facts must be favourable to the appropriateness and fairness of the decision. At all events, it is a poor security for the impartial administration of justice, that the judge lives some hundreds of miles off. Indeed it is difficult to see how the interests of suitors can be promoted by the remoteness of the judge. Litigation is not encouraged by bringing justice to every man's door. On the contrary, nothing would have so great an effect in deterring men from useless disputes, as the certainty that they would be promptly decided. If the delay of justice be the means of diminishing litigation and promoting concord, the legitimate inference is, that the total denial of it would be the very consummation of conciliatory wisdom. It is a most absurd and mistaken notion, that the greater number of lawsuits are undertaken without any reason. Most suits are unquestionably based on a conviction of right; and the more promptly the judge decides whether this conviction be just or erroneous, the better. It is no less a prejudice to regard the compromise of a dispute as invariably the best way of terminating it; it is good only when the demands made are of an extravagant nature. If they are (as they generally are) perfectly fair, justice ought to be awarded them immediately ; and, above all, the complainant ought not to be driven by legal delays to concede any part of his just claims for the advantage of an unjust adversary. Unpaid justice may, like unpaid education, be a doubtful good; but the monstrous expense of English justice is utterly indefensible, and arises, in great measure, from the want of local tribunals. If, for instance, in insignificant revenue causes, the matter is carried from the Orkneys to London*, witnesses, documents, and everything necessary to the conduct of the cause, must also be transmitted thither ; and this (as the advocates of Lord Brougham's bill maintain) involves a complete denial of justice. Some reduction of these costs—indeed an entire abolition of them, in the case of the poor and the innocent—must be effected here as well as in other countries. Lastly, that all juristical wisdom and learning is found in London alone, and decreases or disappears as you recede from the capital, seems to admit of doubt. If, however, it be the case, this centralization, this extinction of all sense of justice and of all legal science in the provinces, is truly lamentable, and affords quite a sufficient argument for the establishment of local tribunals. If all the counsellors of the local courts and the provincial courts of appeal, with their whole judicial apparatus, were suddenly transferred from every part of the Prus-

* Edinb. Rev., li. 115.

sian monarchy to Berlin, it is certain that the city would gain far less than the country would lose.

The more extensively I inquire here, the more frequently I receive the answer:—the real cause of the failure of the plan of a local administration of justice is, that the judges, barristers, attorneys, &c. are settled in London; that London is a more agreeable and profitable residence to them than the country; that they exercise an irresistible power; and that they regard a distribution of justice throughout England as nothing more nor less than a sacrifice of their money, their influence, and their pleasure.

It would be irrational to wonder at this display of prejudice and selfishness in the lawyers; but why so many Lords made common cause with them, alleging no better reasons than those I have quoted above, is less intelligible or defensible.

There was a time when the House of Peers took the lead in all social progress, and fulfilled this, the proper and the highest vocation of an aristocracy. In modern times, unhappily, the idea has taken root, that its essential destination is to obstruct and to maintain. Those who once formed the gallant and glorious advanced guard are now sunk into the timid stragglers, driven along by the troops of the commonalty; getting no thanks for their negative labours; and, it must be confessed, generally deserving none. It is urged on the other hand, that the House of Lords naturally promoted movement so long as the times required it; but since this has gone on with dangerous velocity, the necessities of a former age are exchanged for the very contrary ones.

This inference can be but half true, at the most : for, from the earliest times there has been no want of restless and revolutionary elements in the House of Commons, which were controlled or neutralized by the authority and the prudence of the House of Lords. But it was to its steady, constant advance that it owed this very authority ; it always led, *because* it was always foremost ; and was neither goaded by the precipitation, nor withheld by the tardiness, of certain parties in the Lower House. Excessive resistance and obstruction have caused an incalculable increase of the powers and energies which were too much compressed. The people wanted space and a channel ; —a valve, by which (to use Machiavelli's expression) they might '*Sfogar gli umori ;*' or, in modern English, 'let off the superfluous steam.'

To give an instance or two :—Had the Lords graciously and promptly consented to take the franchise from East Retford and give it to a large city, it would have averted, for an indefinite time, perhaps for ever, the blow they have received from the sweeping Reform Rill. Had they passed the Irish Tithe Bill and done justice to Ireland, the property of the Irish Church would not have been attacked as it has lately been, or, at any rate, would not have decided the fate of a ministry. But, assuming that government will be again conducted on Tory principles, it must be overthrown again and again, so long as it persists in the same course of mere negation and opposition, with regard to corporations, universities, and every other ques.tion involving the changes necessitated by time.

This seems the most convenient place for the mention of another subject: viz., 'Registration's of mortgages and other deeds.' With the exception of the counties of Middlesex and Yorkshire, there does not exist in all England any institution for registration—any legal, general, uniform mode of registering the value of landed property and houses, its privileges and burthens, the purchase money and the charges upon it, &c. &c. To supply this defect, Mr. Campbell moved for leave to bring in a bill on the 16th December, 1830, for a 'General Register of Deeds.' He said, that at present it was impossible to register or to establish any legal title to real property in England without the greatest difficulty, delay, and expense; that, in spite of the utmost care and caution, not only great uncertainties and doubts remained, but frauds of the grossest kind were practicable. In Ireland, a similar institution has existed for a century; in Scotland, since the year 1617; and, in those parts of the empire, creditors and purchasers feel a security which is unknown in England. Where this security is wanting, the purchaser can never buy without risk, and the capitalist is deterred from lending his money on mortgage.

The most weighty objection which was made to Mr. Campbell's plan was, that the centralization of all registration in London would be attended with too much difficulty and expense. To which he replied, that it would diminish expense, facilitate the obtaining of information, render practicable a uniformity of proceeding, &c. But he subsequently consented to have the registration distributed over the cities and counties.

The objections which remained were merely trivial; such as, that there was no experience how such a thing would work,—though there was the favourable experience of almost every nation in Europe, not to mention Scotland and Ireland: that every man's debts would be generally known, —as if credit could not exist without tricks of concealment and mystery, or as if the whole world would crowd to the registration-office from mere idle curiosity: that no man would be able to borrow money on his own individual securities and deeds,—as if these would not be verified and confirmed, and greater security given to the lender.

In short, the bill was three times thrown out by the Lords, without even an attempt at amending any of the details; and this was consequently adduced by writers as conclusive evidence that the estates of three-fourths of the English nobility were mortgaged to Jews and merchants, and that a desire to conceal this fact was the cause of their hostility to the bill.

There may be things in our system of hypothecation which are susceptible of improvement, but on the whole it is a blessing to the country and the people. When I describe here how easily, rapidly, and cheaply the purchase of a

house is concluded in Prussia, my hearers are
astonished, and again point to the loss of influence which the lawyers would sustain by the
introduction of a more equitable and rational
system in England.

LETTER XXX.

Effect of the French Revolution of July in England—Ignorance of Continental Politicians—Prussian Government and People —English independent of French civilization—Law and Prac-: tice of Inheritance—Their Effects — French and English Tumults—Their Differences.

London, May 29th, 1835.

My letter, or if you will my essay, on the Reform. Bill was designed to compress the facts into the smallest possible space, and to elucidate them by some few remarks. That all my readers will be converted to my way of thinking, never did, and never could, enter my head: but I wish to recur to two or three points, in order to rectify mistakes.

Some German political writers are, as it seems,. fixed in the notion that English reform, together with all that results from it, is entirely a consequence of the French revolution of July. They have so often asserted this, because it suits their purpose, and others have so often ·repeated it after them from similar motives, that they have all ended by believing it an indisputable fact,· and a saving article of faith. And· yet, it is entirely false. Certainly the three days produced a great sensation in England, as they did everywhere; but it betrays the most absolute and resolute ignorance of that country, to imagine that the ground-work and matter of English civilization have ever passed over from France; or that the English have ever exhibited the remotest trace of an inclination to ape the Parisians,—as the Belgians were, with some reason, reproached with doing. When the atmosphere is charged with electricity, are there not conductors and nonconductors of the fluid? Why did the three days excite not the slightest agitation through the whole Prussian monarchy? Was it because the police or the censorship put on spectacles of a higher power? Not a whit. It was because the wisdom of the king, and the fidelity of his servants, had long ago removed all the revolutionary matter, which in other countries burst into a flame; because they had reformed in time; because the just demands of the age had been more fully and conscientiously complied with in Prussia, than in any other country in Europe. The three days, then, do not of necessity create revolutions everywhere out of nothing, and about nothing, and against nothing. On the contrary, they confirmed every rational man in Prussia in his conviction of the immense advantages of the gradual progress which had been directed by his own government; and enhanced his love for king and fatherland (especially in the Rhenish provinces) by a comparison with the troubles and the sufferings of other countries. The bigots, who are incessantly representing the revolution of July as an inevitable poison, do but increase the danger, and would indeed import the contagion, if they could succeed in goading the government into

XXX.] FRANCE AND ENGLAND. 81

uncalled-for and illiberal measures, and thus
creating a universal malady by their ill-timed
and pernicious drugs.

Instead of persisting in general abstractions;
instead of throwing London, Paris, Brussels,
Brunswick, Dresden, Warsaw, Athens, and Madrid, all into one pot; instead of tediously reite-
rating the some formulæ, and for ever thrashing
the same straw; it would be more to the purpose
if they would inquire into the varieties of circumstances, the peculiar motives, the causes of attraction or repulsion, and, out of all these symptoms
and experiments, deduce some more profound
and appropriate curative science. A man who
traces all diseases to one cause, or seeks all relief
from one remedy, is, and must ever be, a quack.

All the great moral, intellectual, and political improvements or changes of England have originated
independently of France, and have been effected
in opposition to France; and notwithstanding a
few compliments, which certain writers bandy to
and fro across the Channel, England in all her
most essential characteristics and her most important institutions, is, to this day, *far more German than French.* This will be proved, not, as I
said before, by the incidents of the moment, nor
by a passing conjuncture brought on by a thousand collateral causes; but by the very nature and
necessities of her being.

The revolution of July was the cause neither
of the miseries and the complaints of Ireland,
nor of the disabilities and discontents of the Dissenters, nor of sinecures and pluralities, nor of

high taxes, nor of close corporations, nor of
bigoted and narrow-minded universities: it has
not even thrown the least new light on these
things; it has had no more effect in either dis-
turbing or accelerating the course of England,
than a comet has in changing the course of the
planets. It was not the sight of France; it was the
experience at home,— that Ireland, by her patience
or her respectful petitions, had for centuries obtained no adequate redress; but that, as soon as
she assumed a more passionate and menacing
attitude, even men like Wellington and Peel were
frightened into conceding that, which they ought
long ago to have voluntarily bestowed. And
thus will ill-judged resistance continue to lead
on, at every step, to increased demand. Why
then does school represent *every* demand as
unjust? Why do many in Berlin stigmatize
what the king has done for the good of his people, for the establishment of religious concord
and of civil order, and for the removal of all
grounds or elements of revolution, as papistical,
revolutionary, jacobinical? Such declaimers are
really, what they call others,—revolutionary and
jacobinical. If their views were suffered to prevail, must not everything in Prussia be overturned? must not all that the king has been
doing for thirty years, be abolished? and the
whole system of the legislature be destroyed, in
order to convert the country into a Utopia of
their fashion? Thank God, Prussia is in as little
danger from them, as England! Thank God, the
history of the world is not likely to be read back-

wards to please them, whatever differences of opinion may exist as to the degree of rapidity with which we ought to advance. But even were it true that the revolution of July had exercised ever so strong an influence here, yet what the English have aimed at and have accomplished is so completely different from what the French have either conceived or done, that it would be not the less erroneous to deduce any conclusions as to England from French premises. The common maxim or truism, that men are the same everywhere, subject to the same follies and passions, requires to be qualified and explained by a number of particulars; such as attachment to this or that form of religion, constitution, occupation, &c. &c. I will only advert to a few points,—important, though often overlooked,—by which England is distinguished from almost all other countries.

1.—It is not the letter of the law of inheritance, by which the father is at liberty to dispose of his whole property at his pleasure; but the voluntary practice, as to this matter, which is so peculiar to England, and so full of important results. It raises up, in a manner unknown to France and Germany, a continually renewed race of great landed proprietors;—an unbroken line of aristocrats and conservatives. Nor are these at all confined to peers; the same usage obtains, with the same results, among commoners. Here lies a counterpoise to the increasing power of the democracy, far more effective and weighty than is generally supposed or understood.

2.—So long as this universal practice, which

has grown up with the whole structure of
English manners and habits, continues to prevail, a modified conservative party must always
continue to spring up and to obtain influence.
Instead of the rotten boroughs, the counties will
now be the theatre of its exercise; and the Reform
Bill is-advantageous, and not injurious, to them.
Instead of a narrow and decayed foundation, they
have now a broad and solid one; and instead of
an illegal form, they have now law on their side.
Even the last election proved this, and afforded
an ample confutation of the predictions of an
impending absolute sway of ultra-radicals.

3.—Only the eldest son of a peer is, politically
speaking, noble: all the younger sons are commoners; and since, as before, the Reform Bill,
they can sit in the House of Commons, where
they will naturally act as mediators, and endeavour to avert a collision with the Upper House,
unless the latter obstinately oppose reasonable
measures.

4.—We quiet continentals cannot understand
the noisy and public life of this country. Associations, combinations, processions, petitions signed
by thousands and tens of thousands, meetings,
" strikes," "rows," and all such demonstrations,
appear to us palpable signs of dissolution—be-.
ginnings of a resistless, universal convulsion. But
it is no such thing; and the prophecies founded
upon these facts, or upon the supposed analogy
with the French, have never been fulfilled. Instead of inquiring into the *wherefore*, people
generally go on in the old track, and repeat, one

after another, the hacknied cry, " England is on
the brink of ruin ;"—because the tailors want
higher wages, or the newspapers are vulgar and
violent.

But let us now put aside all this, and attend
to one question, *why* have Parisian tumults generally overturned,—or, at least, greatly shaken—
the government, while those of England have
never produced any serious results ?   There are,
you will say, many and important reasons sufficiently obvious.   But have you ever thought of
this one ?—In England there is no preventive or
anticipative police, as in many countries of Europe, and especially in France.   I shall not now
inquire which system is the best, but shall only
state that this is the fact.   The consequence,
however, of this fact is, that when a tumult
breaks out in Paris, the preventive means are
generally exhausted, and everything rushes into
irretrievable confusion and violence.   In England, on the contrary, the ' *movement*' is suffered to grow and flourish in such unchecked
vigour, that the distant observer expects a similar overthrow.   If the government here were
to attempt to interfere before any overt acts
have been committed, every Englishman, without
exception, would regard this as an invasion of
natural and lawful freedom, and nobody would be
found to support a preventive administration.
But as soon as a commotion comes to a really
dangerous pass—to an open violation of the laws,
—the government steps in with decisive and over-

whelming force, and experiences the most ener-
getic and universal support. What is regarded
abroad as the beginning of a revolution is, in
reality, the crisis; and is, in a very different
sense than in France, *le commencement de la fin.*

LETTER XXXI.

German Commercial League—Prussia, Austria, Hamburg—Exhibition, British Gallery—Covent Garden—Queen's box—Characteristic of Philistines—Journey to Windsor—Miseries, aqua-
tic and acoustic—Presentation to the Queen—Windsor Castle
—Its Grandeur and historical Interest—Shakspeare—Return
to town—B— House—Rout—English Musical Composers.

London, June 1st, 1835.

I SEE, in the newspapers, with great joy, that
Baden has joined the German commercial league.
What, a few years ago, appeared either utterly
impossible, or an oppressive tyranny, gradually
came to be regarded as desirable, but unat-
tainable; and now stands before our eyes as an
inestimable advantage to the whole commercial
population of Germany, and a guarantee for German union and political independence—as an
incentive and an assistance to great and useful
enterprises—a death-blow to innumerable tricks
of rapacity and cunning—a means of keeping
monopolizing neighbours within bounds of moderation—an indissoluble bond of union for the
material and moral interests of all Germans.
Since old prejudices have given way, and better
views have vanquished error and ill will, nobody
doubts that (next to our deliverance from foreign
domination) this great commercial union is the
most fortunate event that has befallen Germany;
the commencement of a new era.   On both occa-

sions Prussia set the first steps; on both, they were daring and dangerous, but honourable. No decisive judgment can be formed of the aggregate results of this measure, on the ground that it will cause some individual loss, or that some changes and modifications of it will be necessary. As its most important objects are accomplished, there can be no doubt that, with care and zeal, particulars may be improved and arranged for the common advantage. The essential thing in this, as in every great political measure, is, that *all* the parties concerned should gain; but those who will cling to every antiquated usage, and cannot get out of their snail's pace, must blame not these new times of freedom and community of trade, but themselves.

Were there but one good result from this measure, viz., that all Germany is stimulated, nay forced, into a common rivalry; that the most industrious, careful, orderly, honourable, and intelligent must take the lead; the advantage would be incalculable, and would shed new light and life over our common fatherland. Those who have given a tardy acquiescence, because they were more capable of understanding petty calculations than comprehensive views or high feelings, must be received, without reproach, as penitent children. But those who obstinately persist in severing themselves—whether out of indolence or selfishness—from the rest of their country, merit not only the pecuniary loss which they will be sure to suffer, but disgrace and reprobation.

I am not so partial or so ignorant as not to

acknowledge the difficulties which lie in the way of some members of the league, especially Austria and Hamburg; but even here, I am persuaded that old forms might be modified and adapted to modern times. I am a Prussian (and a better Prussian than a handful of men who affect a monopoly of patriotism will allow me to be); but it grieves me to the soul that Austria is so dragged away from Germany by the weight of the foreign portions of her empire, and in so many respects isolated and estranged. Yet the same pulse beats in the two ventricles of Germany, Prussia and Austria, and the same vital stream might circulate, unchecked, from Memel and Presburg to Schaffhausen and Trier.

And Hamburg? When I first published my opinion that Leipzig would be a gainer by the adhesion of Saxony to the German commercial league, I was laughed at as a fool. I risk this misfortune a second time; and affirm that the destination of Hamburg is to be the London of Germany (after the decay of Antwerp and Rotterdam). But if she does not understand the times; if she does not seize the right moment; if she chooses rather to be a separate isolated star than a part of the great German planetary system, the petty triumphs of apparent independence will soon vanish, and she will sink into obscurity.

It is to be regretted that many English consider the German commercial league from a one-sided and subordinate point of view. The impulse which originated in Prussia, and had so powerful an effect in inducing a more liberal commercial system in England, now, for the second time, operates for the advantage of both parties.

We will drop all consideration of those who preposterously imagine that England has the right and the power to direct the commercial system of Germany, though they would be the first to treat a similar assumption, on the part of Germans, as madness. We shall then only have to meet the objections of those who think that trade with an inactive and poor nation, is more profitable than trade with one which is growing in activity, wealth, and intelligence. But this position is found to be so untenable—this opinion has been so thoroughly confuted—that it is impossible to drag it forth any more from the lumber-garret of exploded prejudices, even though it be furbished up with new rhetorical patches. Whatever is really advantageous to the German producer, manufacturer, and consumer, is, if regarded from a proper elevation, also advantageous to England. To deny this is to fall back into the doctrine of the utility of restrictions, of monopolies, the 'continental system,' &c. Till somebody has the courage frankly to defend these things, it would be time lost to attack them.

In these and similar errors, however, there is some method; but what shall we say when government *employés* maintain that the abolition of the custom-house restrictions is highly dangerous, because it lessens the supervision of the police, and opens the door for the entrance of political poison? One may say either, Lord, forgive them! for they know not what they do; or, Lord, forgive them

not, for they know right well what they do, and
what they intend. A whole army could not keep
out physical contagion, and moral contagion is to
be excluded by the fly-flapper of a police or custom-house officer posted on the high road! What
disgusting presumption, or what ludicrous fool-
ery, with and concerning history and revolution—
the content and discontent of nations! Prussia
is so healthy and happy, in consequence of the
king's timely and beneficent reforms, that she
may let these insects buz unheeded. If there
were cause and matter for revolutionary troubles,
these prophets of ill would sink back, in the first
stadium, into that region out of which a chance
ray of sun has warmed them into life.

June 2nd, 1835.

I went, at ten o'clock, with M—— and M——,
to a picture-gallery of a twofold sort. Every
year the wealthy possessors of pictures lend some
out of their collections, to form an exhibition,
which is open to the public by day, and to a numerous but select company in the evening, when
the room is brilliantly lighted with gas. The
tickets for the day are sold; those for the evening
given. This custom is very liberal and laudable,
and for many years a new and attractive exhibition has been annually furnished from these
stores. This is sufficient to show how many
works of art there are in England, and how poor
most other nations would appear in the comparison. On the other hand, it must be said, that,
generally speaking, the English have got no fur-

ther than the possession of them; and that the pleasure and fame of producing has been chiefly left to others. I saw some admirable landscapes of Ruysdael, Holbein, Both, &c.: a beautiful Venus by Paul Veronese, a very remarkable Mantegna, two Rembrandts (a Bürgermeister and his wife, and Rembrandt's Mother), both of the highest merit; a few Titians (some of which might have been taken for Bonifacios), Murillos, and a great number of Flemish paintings. But Waagen will give you a much more circumstantial account of all this.

The living pictures, that is the ladies, formed the other half of the exhibition; and this time the beautiful and the ugly were so mixed, that the contrasts were the more marked and striking.

June 3rd, 1835.

Having finished my work, and paid a few visits, I dined with Waagen at B——n v. B——'s. We then drove to Covent Garden, as the Queen had most graciously lent us her box. We saved our time at the door, and our money in our pockets, and saw much better than in the places accessible to us: but what did we see and hear?—At the end of the opera 'Lestocq,' a burning palace, and a mighty firing with little cannons. Auber's music was thoroughly unmeaning, and the singing (with the exception of Mr. Seguin) no better; nevertheless the public signified its approbation several times. The time seemed long to me, and I renounced the pleasure of seeing whatever was to be seen between the hours of eleven and one o'clock.

London, June 4, 1835.

It is a peculiar and almost infallible characteristic of Philistines, that when the greatest, noblest, and most beautiful that nature or art, government or science has produced, is shown to them, they say, with the quiet air of perfect self-complacency, ' Dear me, I thought the mountains were higher, the ships larger, the streets longer, voices stronger, suns brighter, stars more numerous, wisdom wiser, justice more just, courage more courageous, temperance more temperate.' And what *did* they really think? Just nothing at all. But they inflate themselves with the emptiness of the heart and spirit. Their vigour of thought and feeling always turns out to be an abstract negation. According to that, the fellow in ' Tieck,' who says, ' Tell me the greatest number and I will imagine a still greater,' is the profoundest of mathematicians. The most beautiful, delightful, and memorable days of one's life are those in which reality surpassed vague expectation, and gave a form and meaning to things which our own imagination could never have perfectly embodied.

   *   *   *   *   *

But whither am I wandering, with an introduction which is fit for the second part of my yesterday's history, but not at all for the first? ' You must be here at half-past nine,' said the coach-proprieter as he booked my name for Windsor.

I was on the spot with my usual punctuality;
not so the coach; and when it at last arrived,
some gentlemen had already taken possession of
the best places, those behind the coachman. I
had only the choice left me of sitting behind,
with my face to the horses, but without anything
against my back (for the iron bar which sur-
rounds it, four inches above the seat, can hardly
be called a resting-place), or opposite, with my
back to the horses, but secured from falling over
backwards and breaking my neck. I chose the
latter, but found the seat very hard and narrow.
Having made this observation, the coachman
brought me a cushion to sit on, which so much
delighted me that I bore the discomfort of waiting more patiently than usual, and only looked
with annoyance at the thick fog which rendered it
utterly impossible to see any thing, and threatened
soon to change into deluges of rain. But, contrary
to my expectations, the first wet did not come from
above but from below—*destillatio per ascensum.*
The cushion, a gift so welcome at first, was
swelled up like a sponge with the rain of the
preceding night, and imparted to me a most un-
endurable portion of its contents. Dry straw was
laid on the cushion to depose this supremacy of
water, but in vain; though I kept as still as I
could, the straw escaped to the right and left, and
I sank down again into the primeval waters, until
my only deliverance lay in coat-tails and pocket-
handkerchiefs.

At length we started.—And now a new misery.
Behind me stood a large hamper filled with

pewter plates and pots, which, with Logierian steadiness and perseverance, executed a thema, known and loved for centuries in the pot-houses of England. These Orphic tones soon exercised their wonted power on the basket in which they were imprisoned. It fell into the motion appropriate to its semi-pyramidal form, and beat time with such regularity on my shoulders that I was compelled to respond, however unmusically inclined.

Meanwhile a soft rain began to fall, and gave a new turn to my thoughts and sensations. The expanded umbrella altered the position of the centre of gravity; and I should gladly have recalled my old Halle university learning, concerning the lever, the hypomochlion, and whatever else might be applicable to the case.

Amid these and other curious speculations I reached Windsor, and hastened to pay my respects to Dr. H——. The grand thing, however, was, that Waagen and I were to be presented to the queen.

Friday, June 5, 1835.

The English newspapers have said (and what will they not say?) that the queen is an *intrigante* in politics. As soon as I saw her, I was ready to take my historical oath that this is not true. Her whole appearance is expressive of the greatest good humour and of true German simplicity. As she showed me the pictures of her father and her relations, and said to me, 'Now you must see my room,' I could not indeed forget what personage was speaking, surrounded as I saw her; and yet this very personage—this queen—made an impression upon me which more vividly recalled not only fatherland, but house and home, than any English woman I have seen. Most assuredly I did not get up any artificial impression; it came unexpectedly and spontaneously. So much the more do I want an explanation, 'Whence these accusations arise?' The following appears to me a natural one.

The queen has her own opinion on politics as well as on other subjects, but, from inclination and from principle, will not interfere, or play any part in public affairs. But politics obtrude themselves into her domestic circle, and she is perhaps called upon to change her personal attendants (with whom she is familiar and satisfied) with every change or wish of the ministry. This must be peculiarly and supremely disagreeable to a German princess; and those by whom she is surrounded, whose opinions are more decided and violent, may have taken advantage of it to represent their royal mistress as a centre of certain opinions and intrigues. As the Tories did this to strengthen themselves, their adversaries would equally overstep the bounds of truth in their indignation and abuse.

Perhaps this history *à priori* which I am writing is more veracious than a vast many histories *à posteriori*.

Lord H——— very obligingly showed us the whole of the castle, much more than is usually shown; and this brings me to the introduction of this letter. Windsor far exceeded my expectations, and made a greater impression on me than all the other castles I have ever seen, put together. It combines the bold originality of the middle ages with the 'highest pitch of splendour and comfort which our times can reach. It is not an empty, tedious, monotonous repetition of the same sort of rooms, over and over again; but every staircase, every gallery, every room, every hall, nay, every window, is different, surprising, peculiar; in one word, poetical. In the rich, busy, hurrying London, I have often longed for the quiet of decaying Venice,—often looked for a tinge of poetic melancholy, or of fantastic originality. In vain; no trace was to be found even in society. Always the sharp outline of reality; the mathematics of life; the arts of calculating, of gaining, of governing. In Windsor, on the contrary, England's history, so rich in interest, with all its recollections, suddenly stands before my eyes. These gigantic towers, bastions, balconies, chapels, churches, and knightly halls in fresh and boundless variety; at every step new views over rivers, valleys, woods, and fields; the fancies of a thousand years crowded together into one instant, and far surpassing everything that Opera decorators would dare to represent on paper and canvass.

I could understand Versailles, and see Louis the Fourteenth and his court walking up and down in the straight rectangular walks among the formal hedges, fountains, and half-fabulous animals: it was just a scene from Racine or Corneille. In Windsor, for the first time since I was in

England, I fully understood that Shakspeare was
an Englishman. Here he reigns as monarch,
and his romantic world here finds a local habita-
tion. As we were afterwards whirled along in
the royal carriage through the green meadows,
and among the ancient oaks and beeches, where
the wildest nature is interspersed with beautiful
gardens and quiet lakes, and where richly-orna-
mented boats lay ready moored to transport us to
the distant wooded and mysterious shore, I felt
that I was on the spot where the Henrys reigned,
and acted their great and gorgeous tragedies;
where, in moonlight nights, Oberon and Titania
sport with their fairy troops; where Rosalind
wanders in the forest, or Jaques indulges in his
melancholy musings, or Beatrice throws out her
keen jests like bright arrows.

When the weather had stormed itself out we
drove home through the richly-cultivated country.
it was a beautiful evening and we could see
farther than usual; but as soon as we got near
London we were surrounded with a thick fog:
a grey curtain hid from us the garden of poetry,
and the prose of life demanded a dinner at nine
o'clock at night.

*   *   *   *   *   *   *

The day was fertile enough, without any ap-
pendix; but a card, 'Lady F. E—— at home,' imposed new duties upon me. On entering, at half-
past eleven, I found four persons, and assuming
that these were members of the family, I was the

first guest. Let us forget my hymn to Windsor,
and I can then call this spacious palace, adorned
with the finest pictures, princely, nay regal.
Among the female part of the company there
were many who surpassed the creations of art.
Why should none of them possess the talent, the
wit, the humour, the sensibility, the originality,
the melancholy, the gaiety, which Shakspeare
found on English ground, and glorified by his
genius? But truly a 'rout' is not the place to
unfold the wings of soul or body; and in this
stately and splendid reality the greatest poetical
vigour is compressed into a mathematical point.
How much I wished for the talisman in Madame
de Genlis' ' Palais de la Vérité,' that I might see
what lay hidden in head or heart under these pearls
and diamonds; how much I longed to try whether
they would return any echo worthy of the music
of Shakspeare. After I, black atom, had humbly
wound my way for an hour among these dazzling
forms, I was at last compelled to recollect that I
had been above eighteen hours in motion. The
ladies who were still waiting in their carriages for
the possibility of alighting, remained concealed
from my outward eyes; with my inward, I turned
back to Shakspeare's noble and lovely creations,
till dream and reality blended, as in Windsor.

*   *   *   *   *   *   *

Yesterday I was obliged to take a sort of holi-
day; for too great exertions depress the spirits.
This is the more necessary, because, after my

harvest at the Museum, I am come upon dry stubble-fields. I spent the whole day and the evening in reading and writing.

The only piece of information worth mentioning is what I heard the other day from Mr. E. Taylor concerning the modern English composers. He spoke with great truth of the danger of an exclusive taste; he complained very justly that people were often ignorant of the productions of past times, and negligent of those of their own country: but, on the other hand, patriotism cannot make something out of nothing. Why does all Europe acknowledge and honour and admire the poets, the statesmen, the orators of England? Why does it know almost nothing of her painters and her musicians? Why do we see the very contrary with regard to Germany and Italy? A German who is not acquainted with all the great English poets, from Shakspeare to Byron and Scott, is very justly reproached; but,—heaven forgive me my ignorance!—I did not know the name of one of the composers I heard praised, with the exception of Mr. Bishop; and yet I am not the most ignorant neither. Who, in Berlin, ever heard of Shield, Cooke, Steevens, Spofforth, Horsley, Attwood, Goss, &c.?

Certainly the lyrical part of music is important, but will as little suffice to found a great musical school upon, as portrait painting in the sister art. Several specimens of the compositions of these gentlemen were so much alike, that they showed the character of a school, if you will, but a school of which one does not find the master. From him must flow the main stream; if this is wanting, the numerous little streamlets of the scholars do little for the history of art, and dry up in a season. These pieces all wore the same colouring—a sentimentality bordering on sickliness: I thought them very inferior to any thing that Reichardt and Zelter had produced—not to mention the great masters.

LETTER XXXII.

Sir R—— P——,Mr. O'Connell—German Demagogues—Hay-
market Theatre; Royal Box—Much Ado about Nothing—
Concert—Musical Criticism—Zoological Gardens—Society of
Arts — English Parties — Chantrey — Sculpture — State-Paper
Office—Hanover-Square Concert—Messiah.

London, June 5th, 1835.

I CONCLUDED my last letter, a few hours ago,
with the remark that, probably, the next day
would produce nothing remarkable. Since I wrote
that, I have paid two visits which would alone
repay the trouble of a journey, and which render
the present day one of the most memorable I
have passed in England. Sir R—— P—— had
asked the B—n B—— what degree of reliance
was to be placed on the accuracy of an article
which had appeared in an English journal on our
municipal system. B—— v. B—— referred him
to me, and, armed with á letter of introduction,
I called upon him.

The room into which I was shown bespoke
both wealth and taste. The walls were covered
with book-shelves filled with the choicest books;
works of art stood about, and an exquisite little
statue of Venus occupied me till Sir R. P——
entered. He has something, I am tempted to
say, German in his exterior; he is not so tall and
slender as many Englishmen; he holds the 'juste

milieu' between the leanness of Pitt and the ro-
tundity of Fox.   His enunciation is so clear and
distinct that I understood every word.   On my
part, it was easier to me to speak with a statesman on grave and important topics, than with
house-maids and waiters on those with which they
are conversant.   At least, I could find means to
make myself intelligible concerning the main
features of our institutions.   '

To-day the new municipal system is to be dis- ·
cussed, and Sir R. P—— said, he wished to have
some conversation with me after he knew what
turn the debate would take.   I replied, that I
should always be ready to attend his summons,
and that I esteemed it a great pleasure to make
his acquaintance.   And indeed, but for this opportunity, I should never have ventured to obtrude myself on this remarkable man.

Grown bolder, I bethought myself—a foreigner
is free to ask more than one question of fate and
of great men; and I suddenly conceived the
project of going straight from P—— to his
antagonist,—to—(H—— will be furious) — to
Daniel O'Connell.   I found him in a small room,
sitting at a writing table covered with letters,
in his dressing gown.   I began with apologies
for intruding upon him without any introduction,
and pleaded my interest in the history and fate '
of Ireland, and in his efforts to serve her.   When
I found that he had read my historical letters, I ,
felt on a better footing.   I could not implicitly ·
accept his opinion concerning Elizabeth (which
he has borrowed from Lingard) as a good bill.

We agreed, however, on the subject of the much disputed and much falsified history of the Ca-'tholic conspiracy of 1641. I refer you for my opinions to my narrative of this event in the fifth volume of my history of Europe. I am also per-'fectly of his opinion that the tenants at will—those Lassi*—are in a worse condition in Ireland than any where; and that, both with regard to moral and intellectual culture, or physical prosperity, their position is not comparable to that of our thrice-happy proprietary peasants. I told him that what he desired for Ireland had long been possessed by the Catholics of Prussia; and that hatred and discontent had expired with persecution.

The English ministry first made this man a giant; but he is a giant, too, by the strength of his own mind and will, in comparison with the Lilliputians cut out of reeds, which we call demagogues; and which are forced to be shut up in the Köpenick hot-house, or put under a Mainz forcing-glass, to rear them into any size and consideration. But for this careful tending, these rushes would long ago have been dried up and whirled away by the wind; now, at least, we have the satisfaction of preserving some in our political herbariums, *in perpetuam rei memoriam.* Thank God, however, the governments of Germany do not prepare the ground for universal discontent; if this prevailed, and prevailed with justice, O'Connells must of necessity arise.

They would be touched by the sufferings of

* A name for slaves or serfs in the middle ages.—*Translator.*

their country; they would be exasperated by the
injustice done to her, till the storm of excitement
would naturally tear down the obstacles wantonly
opposed, and conquer by violence what had been
denied to reasonable prayers.

London, June 6th, 1835.

Your dissertation on the greatness or smallness
of German demagogues (I hear you say) is quite
superfluous; you had much better have described
to us what that arch agitator and rebel, O'Connell,
looks like.—What he looks like? A tall, gaunt
man, with a thin face, sunken cheeks, a large
hooked nose, black piercing eyes, malignant
smile round the mouth, and, when in full dress,
a cock's feather in his hat, and a cloven foot.
" That is just what I imagined him," cries one.
But, as it happens, that is just what he is not.
On the contrary, he has a round, good-natured
face. In Germany he would be taken for a
good, hearty, sturdy, shrewd farmer; indeed he
distinctly reminded me of the cheerful, sagacious,
and witty old bailiff Romanus, in Rotzis.

*   *   *   *

The Queen yesterday sent a ticket for the royal
box at the Haymarket Theatre, for Waagen and
me. I am not accustomed to such grandeurs as
royal boxes and carriages; and only once in my
life (at Windsor) have sentinels presented arms
to me, and people stared at me in consequence.
And then it seemed to me as if I were sitting
there to be laughed at, or were acting the interlude in Shakspeare's ' Taming of the Shrew.'
Yesterday, at the Haymarket, I sat hidden

behind the green curtain; and as we two were alone in the box, the greatest possible comfort was superadded to other advantages. Indeed, in despite of my very humble station, I am quite spoiled with regard to the theatre; and when I have not a comfortable place secured to me, my artistical enthusiasm cools. Waiting, crowding, and elbowing are democratic joys, which always excite my longing for the aristocratic seclusion of a stall. So I sat in the Haymarket on the royal seat (but without Damocles' sword over my head); and saw, first, ' The Village Lawyer,' a farce with three prominent parts, which were very well and amusingly represented by Webster, Buckstone, and Strickland. Then followed ' Much ado about Nothing,' acted in romantic costume, and without the absurd modernising of the torturers. In spite of this, the piece, acted in London and by Eng-lishmen, did not produce upon me the effect that it did in Germany.

I cannot get accustomed to the manner of speaking and acting here. This strong accentu-ation, this pointed division of syllables, these violent contrasts, these commas between every word, this smothering of the voice so that the round full volume of sound is entirely lost, this screaming out, and these changes of tone—I can see, in all this, nothing but mannerism, which, however, seems to be as much admired, and in-deed to deserve it as much, as the violent sfor-zando and diminuendo, the transitions and the tricks, of the present Italian school of singing.

Moreover, I had great difficulty in connecting

the separate scenes of Benedict into one human whole ; they were *disjecta membra* of affected seriousness and broad comedy. Ought not his witty and brilliant insolence, under which is hidden so amiable a character, to be brought into one homogeneous and synchronous being ? Miss Taylor acted her part cleverly, but it was all acting ; and I saw only the taught performer, instead of the poetical form of a maiden, who is resistless as soon as she tempers the keenness of her wit with the least grain of generous and gentle affection.

I may be mistaken, but it did not appear to me that Shakspeare conceived these most poetical characters as Kemble and Miss Taylor play them. How refined and elegant was Wolf, even in his bitterest speeches ; how far removed from any descent to low comedy; how he combined keenness with good humour, and a kind of self-irony, which unconsciously offers itself to raillery, and meets it half-way! The same of Beatrice : her towering, haughty spirit is not forced up by a steam-press, nor has she any deliberate intention of giving pain ; it bursts forth at her fingers' ends, and is a real overflow of wit and talent, whose brilliant coruscations only conceal the core of a heart not only capable of love and of friendship, but unconsciously teeming with both, and therefore doubly engaging. Thus did Mlle. F——, whom I last saw as Beatrice, conceive the character ; thus have several German actresses represented it. Here, on the contrary, it struck me, what cold bitter quarrels the ill-joined couple would fall into, and how they would curse the jest which had transformed them, against their natures, into husband and wife!

Sunday, June 7th, 1835.

As I am so much in the vein of a *frondeur* and a critic, I will e'en go on, and not be chary of my heresies.

Yesterday evening I heard a 'Grand Selection' of music, sacred and profane, at Drury-lane. About thirty pieces were sung, of which I heard twenty-two; the third act, in which Rossini reigned paramount, I gave into the bargain.

The performance began with some of the airs and choruses out of Beethoven's 'Mount of Olives,' and here begin my heresies. All that I saw and heard yesterday (and on former occasions) bears the character of instrumental and not of vocal music, is imperfectly adapted to the words, and does not in the slightest degree affect me in the way I require and expect from sacred music. Even what followed, out of 'Haydn's Seasons,' was sacrosanct in comparison with Beethoven.

Weber's Overture to 'Oberon' is characteristic of the author—full of sensibility, genius, and melody. But had I as much time for criticising as I have inclination, I should try to show that an overture ought not to be a pot-pourri;—a cento of melodies taken from the most unlike situations or passages of the opera, and lightly stitched together. This sort of patchwork cannot combine the disconnected, incongruous parts into a true whole; at the very best it is only

intelligible *after* the opera; and in that case it is
not an overture, nor is it possible for a conception of the whole opera to be crowded together
in this manner.   Gluck and Spontini never attempted this; and the sort of echoes of motivi
that are found in some of Mozart's overtures
are essentially different from Weber's mode of
treatment in his 'Euryanthe' and 'Oberon.' When
I heard the latter, however, yesterday, I was affected with melancholy, at the early death of this
pure and noble-minded man, in the solitude of
London, far from family and friends.

Rossini's celebrated Preghiera came between
Handel's ' Holy, holy Lord God Almighty' and
' Sound an alarm.' How empty, bare, trivial, and
flat did the flimsy manufacture of the Italian
Maestro appear, in comparison with the profound
thought and feeling of the German Meister! At
each of these alternations, which occurred very
frequently, I could not help thinking of Aris-
tophanes' balance of the merits of Euripides and
Æschylus.   The scale of Rossini rose far higher
in comparison than that of Euripides; it was
only in the comic parts that his talent was pre-
dominant.

The singing was perfectly suited to the com-
position; Grisi, especially, displayed her skill in
these musical *tours de force*,—in this dancing on
stilts, and jumping through a hoop.   The English
know the value of a pound sterling in most things,
but they seem to be quite dazzled by the glitter of
these gilded maravedis, and to be guilty of injustice towards their native artists.   The simple

utterance of a touching air of Handel's, by Miss
Kemble, went more to my heart than all the
tricks à la Tartini, or à la Rossini.   It is to be
hoped that Miss Kemble will not fall into the
common mistake of thinking that the school of
fashion is the school of art; or estimate these
gross departures from a truly feminine mode of
singing—these mere instrumental solfeggios—as
the highest proof of merit.   May she never lay
aside the few pure and perfect pearls of tone
which become her so well, to trick herself out
with loads of false and borrowed jewels.   They
will never produce the same effect on her as on
her Italian rivals.   To each his own.

The voices of the English women, whom I
have heard here, are not comparable in flexibility,
brilliancy, power, and energy, to those of many
Italians.   The English are the voices to marry;
the Italian are like seductive mistresses, whose
syren tones witch away one's senses.   But after a
season, a reasonable man returns to his simple
and natural wife, and to the repose and purity of
home.

As an Englishman near me was admiring the
famous duet from 'Semiramis,' in which the son
learns the murder of his father, and the criminal
love of his mother, I was so indignant, that I
summoned up all my English, in order to prove
to him the absurdity, as well as the revolting
character, of this pretended dramatic music;—
probably without the least effect.   And for this
reason, and to avoid stoning, I will reduce my
audacious pen to silence.

Monday, June 8.

Yesterday, when I had ended my report on English agriculture, and had paid visits with Mr. L. and M., I went to the Zoological Gardens. I have already extolled the laying out of the grounds, and the very complete and well-arranged collection of animals. But yesterday I could not attend to the plants and animals;—the whole garden was filled with people; and the ground before the monkey's cage, or rather palace, was so crowded that one could scarcely make one's way. The chief pleasure consisted in looking at the women: in spite of a good many blanks, they exhibited as brilliant and beautiful a display as the flower-beds. At least as many carriages were in attendance on this select and fashionable company, as drove up and down Longchamps on the three celebrated days, and an equal number was moving at the same time in Hyde Park. So much does the greatness and wealth of London exceed that of all other cities, and that of England all other countries! Meanwhile I walked about, more contented and happy in my poverty than the son of Tippoo Saib, whom I saw, dressed in oriental costume, and accompanied by two very obliging Englishmen. On the other hand, the Asiatic prince was less to be pitied than a pre-eminent dandy would have been, could he have looked behind him and seen that the seam of his coat had burst, and that a black and melancholy-looking shirt was seeking the bleaching rays of the sun through the aperture.

Tuesday, June 9,.

*   *   *   *

At half-past two this sight was over; and I hastened to Exeter Hall, in the Strand, where the annual distribution of the prizes of the Society for the Encouragement of Arts, Manufacture, and Commerce took place—Admiral Sir Edward Codrington in the chair. Though I am accustomed to numerous assemblages, and especially to the great preponderancy of ladies at those held in the mornings—that is, in the evenings—I was astonished. The Hall contained more persons than the floor of the Opera House of Berlin, and at least five-sixths of them were of the female sex. There were certainly not less than eight hundred women—more, perhaps, than I ever saw assembled in one spot. The greater part of the Hall formed a sort of parterre, on one side of which was an amphitheatre of raised benches. After a number of prizes for improvements and inventions in agriculture, mechanics, chemistry, &c., had been distributed, it came to the turn of the arts; and I now discovered why the female portion of the company was even larger than usual. Ladies of various ages received prizes (silver and gold medals) for original drawings and paintings. The gallant distributor took infinite pains to say something obliging to each; and these compliments were received with great applause by the male part of the audience. My curiosity was excited, and I went down from the platform to obtain a view of the works of art hung in front of it. And what did I see? The

very worst thing in our exhibitions is superior to
the best here; and the little dogs and cats, and
heads and flowers, would not have done much credit to a drawing-school.   One of your drawings,
dear ——, would have driven the whole troop of
medalled ladies out of the field.

About a short repose—that is, after lying on
the sofa, and reading the directions for the Lon
don police officers—I went to dine at Mrs. S——'s,
where I was introduced to Miss Aikin, the author
of several historical works, and especially one on
Elizabeth.   She is a well-informed and lively
woman, and I found her conversation very entertaining.

About half-past eleven in the evening I drove
to Sir R. P——'s.   I found an extremely select
company assembled in a room covered with beautiful pictures, and by no means so crowded as I
have seen and described on former occasions.
There existed, therefore, a possibility of going
from one to another, and also of conversing.   It
is my constant custom to endeavour to make
myself at home in what is new and strange to
me, and to discover the grounds of it.   Though,
therefore, I must regard over-crowded parties as
ill-judged and exceptional, I can perceive that
very numerous ones are, to some persons, inevitable.   If they were to attempt to receive their
visitors in small instalments, the whole year would
not suffice.   The number of acquaintances and of
parties naturally increases with the vastness of the
town, the elevation in society, wealth and eminence
of the host; and if I find myself obliged to exceed

the number of the Muses in my parties at No. 67, Kochstrasse, I can see that certain persons must be compelled to go .beyond that of the Danaids. However, it is not the less true, that every body has the power of giving into this more or less, and that many do it merely from slavish imitation. At one o'clock I went home, satisfied once more with a day so full of amusement and instruction.

Wednesday, June 10.

Yesterday, after. breakfasting with Mr. M——, the son, we visited the studio of the celebrated sculptor, Chantrey. If I compare his works with those of his predecessors, it is impossible. not to perceive (as I remarked in my letter .on Westminster Abbey) an amazing advance; a' return from affectation, exaggeration, and absurdity, to the simplicity of nature—to human attitudes and to the repose which sculpture demands. But this return to nature is only the indispensable preliminary condition—not the highest *aim* of art. By far the greater number of Chantrey's works are busts, or portrait statues (remarkable, as I am assured, for the perfection of the resemblance), and sepulchral monuments, generally conceived with a view to the same end. But I see in these heads merely the faithful impression and imitation of nature; not the poetical and artistical idealization which. nobody can fail to be struck with in the great masters. Likeness, Portrait, is, and must ever be, something one-sided, subordinate, dependant, in art. Men like Lysippus, Raphael, and Titian had the power of breaking down and obli-.

terating the barriers which separate the Real from the Ideal—imitation from creation—and of purifying the given form from all dross, in the refining fire of their genius. If you compare Titian's Charles V. and Adamberger's Charles V. you will have a clear conception of what I mean of what I looked for, and did *not* find. In the whole-length statues of heroes, statesmen, &c., I found, not indeed the defects of the last age, but a certain pervading monotony of the attitude, the station, the draperies, which made me doubt whether I might venture to conclude with certainty that the work gave the precise individuality of the man;—a doubt which cannot by possibility occur to any body who looks at Rauch's Blücher and Scharnhorst.

. All Chantrey's works lie on this side the line beyond which lay the whole region of art among the Greeks: at which beauty of form, and the Ideal (in the true sense of the word) appear as the proper scope of art—the true object of the genial artist. Canova may have his defects; but he attempted to create a Paris, a Perseus, a Venus, and Graces. I do not mention the creations of the German masters. Rauch's two queens far surpass, both in conception and execution, all that I saw in that style at Chantrey's. As to works whose exclusive aim is the revelation of that beauty with which the soul of every artist should be filled,—it were idle to hope that such can ever be produced in a country where the time and thoughts of a popular artist are engrossed by commissions of a very different character.

Many have been of opinion that the unqua-
lified striving after the Beautiful leads to want of
character and to coldness, inasmuch as it is apt
to degenerate into a vague generality. But the
Greek artists demonstrated the contrary in their
gods and goddesses, and elevated even por-
traiture to that point at which it first deserves
the name of art. Most portraits are indeed more
fitted to illustrate a genealogical tree than a history of art.

From Chantrey's studio, I went to call on a
lawyer, Mr. E——, to whom Mr. S—— R—— had
given a little account I had drawn up of our municipal system, and who was desirous of receiving
more detailed information on various points. The
conversation gradually turned on a number of
interesting subjects—crime, punishment, agriculture, &c. I daily find confirmation of my views
and extension of my knowledge. The present
will make me false to the past, if to-morrow does
not pass somewhat differently from to-day.

Thursday, June 11th, 1835.

I am predestined and determined to spend
four hours—from eleven till three—every day,
beginning from yesterday, till my departure from
London, in the State-Paper Office. Since this
most liberal permission was given, I have uniformly been received in the kindest and most
obliging manner. The correspondence which
England has for centuries carried on with the
other European states, and indeed with the most
distant nations,—for example with Abyssinia,—is

at my disposal (the most recent only being, of course, excepted); and I have here occupation for years, so that I might be tempted to stay on and forget my home. It is remarkable, that whilst, wherever I have been, every possible assistance has been given to my historical researches; that whilst even access to the papal archives was granted me, at —————— I have hitherto been excluded from everything that interests me. This is the result, not of illiberal principles, but of antiquated regulations, bad arrangements, and insufficient functionaries. Here, the folios of each country stand well bound, and arranged according to date, on handsome shelves, so that I have only to stretch out my hand to find the information I want. Here, one is not obliged to solicit anything as a favour; here, no unhistorical varlet plays the historical master. In order to add the early part of the reign of Frederick II. to my extracts from Mitchell, I began by the diplomatic correspondence with Berlin, in 1740.

In the evening I heard the ' Messiah' performed by the Royal Society of Musicians, in the room in Hanover Square. This society has existed ever since the year 1738, nearly a century, and has rendered great services to the art, by supporting poor musicians and their widows and orphans. In the year 1834 their receipts from the interest of their funds, donations, regular subscriptions, and concerts, amounted to the large sum of 2749*l*.

If I had more time I could say much about

the general performance and the treatment of particular passages, but I must confine myself to a few observations. There was a sort of prelude on the organ before the several parts or acts, the effect of which was not very grand or solemn, mingled as it was with the tuning of instruments. On the other hand, a very good effect was produced by the organ accompanying and strengthening the choruses. Handel's original score was generally used. Here and there, only, the new instrumentation was adopted in particular parts. Some pieces, for example, 'Every Valley,' were quicker; others, as 'He was despised,' and 'Thy rebuke hath broken his heart,' slower, than with us. I think we hold the just mean. The orchestra and choir were quite powerful enough to fill the room. With us a choir four times as strong, numerically, is not at all louder than this; and here lies the most material point of difference between the performance in London and in Berlin. If, with us, many sing feebly, and some of the young girls only sigh out a timid whisper, it may truly be said that here all, both men and women, sing and scream with might and main. In order to venture upon this, they must certainly be well trained and practised, and sure of their business; still, even then, the general effect is hard and rough. Although I sat on the fourteenth bench from the orchestra, the loudness was so painful to me, that I could hardly sit it out, though used enough to loud music. This is intimately connected with the fact, that all the alto, and the greater part of the soprano, is sung by men and boys; whereas the softness, delicacy, and beauty of our choruses is, in a great measure, the result of the large proportion of female voices. Nor would even these produce so good an effect, were they not regularly practised once or twice a-week the year through. The great excellence of our academy of singing is founded mainly on this unwearied diligence, and on the discrimination and taste to which it gives birth; their choruses are not inferior to this in power, and very superior in beauty, finish, and harmony.

The solo voices were of very different degrees of excellence : the finest, and best suited to the music, was, perhaps, that of Mrs. Knyvett, in the air ' But thou didst not leave.' The most unpleasant that of Mr. Terrail, a short, fat man, who piped out the alto songs, such as ' He was despised.'

Generally speaking, the English singers, male and female, sang with proper simplicity, and only two or three were seduced into the impertinence of foreign cadenzas. On the whole I must give the preference unequivocally to the Berlin performance ; and you, at least, will pardon me for claiming a right to a vote on this matter, as an impartial musical critic of long standing.

LETTER XXXIII.

Uniforms — Orders — Police — Want of popular Amusements —
  Civilization by means of Art — Modern French Drama —
  English Parties—Society—Spirit of Association—Clubs.

London, June 11*th,* 1835.

NOTHING is perhaps more striking to a Berliner,
than the almost total absence of uniforms and
orders in England. Were these the only proofs,
or the only rewards, of merit, either the English
would make a poor figure, or the government
would lie under the reproach of not acknowledging
and rewarding services. Orders certainly have
one great advantage: they present a very cheap
and yet honourable manner of rewarding and
distinguishing merit of all sorts. But this advantage entirely vanishes as soon as they are
given profusely, or without some very especial
reason, and a strict examination into the facts.
Indeed, they should only be granted with the
consent of the most eminent members of the
order. If these indispensable conditions are lost
sight of, orders sink into the region of childish
vanity and petty ambition, till at length their
cheapness renders them despicable. If we were
imperceptibly to arrive at this pitch, it would be
best to call them all in, like bad money, re-coin

them, and issue them afresh. Although in England (for from that I began), they have, numerically, no weight at all, yet for that very reason
they are much more important than with us.

On the other hand, the old subject of praise—
that there is no police to be seen—has become
quite false. In my opinion, however, the praise
was wholly misapplied, and the new police regulations are a great gain, especially for London.
The policemen are plainly dressed in blue without any colour or marks, with the exception of
letters and numbers on the collar, and are apparently unarmed; they have, however, a staff
weighted with lead, which, if required, can do
very effectual service. The regulations of the
service are so rational and so moderate, and the
behaviour of the men employed so exemplary,
that the former prejudices against them have disappeared, although perhaps an instance of individual misconduct may now and then occur.

In the orders, the prevention of crime is de-
signated as the main object; next to that, the
discovering and arresting the criminal after the
crime has been committed.

With respect to police, London is divided
into five districts, each district into five sections,
each section into eight beats. There is a superintendent for each division, under him are five
inspectors, sixteen sergeants, and nine times sixteen constables. None of them are allowed to
appear without the full uniform. The acceptance
of money, under any pretext whatever, is most
strictly forbidden. The constables receive 19s.

per week besides their uniform, which is renewed every year. They serve in particular divisions, and at fixed hours of the day and night, so that they supply the place of watchmen. According to the regulations, the constable is to make himself accurately acquainted with the local and personal circumstances of his beat. His powers and duties, particularly with reference to arrests, are also most accurately defined; and it is said in express words, that "no quality is more indispensable for a policeman than a perfect command of temper." He must on no account allow himself to be irritated by abuse and threats; for if he calmly and firmly does his duty, he will generally induce the by-standers to help him, if necessary.

Every shop or place in which coffee, tea, or other drinks are prepared and sold must be shut at eleven o'clock.

London, June 12, 1835.

How much I have wished that this latter regulation had been extended to the higher classes!

If the working people, who have generally no means of excitement or amusement at command during the week; for whom even Sunday, stern and rigid as it is here, brings no recreation or enjoyment; if they resort to the stimulus of beer and gin, there is an universal cry of horror. It is as far as east from west from all my tastes and opinions to justify this bestial vice; I have but indicated whence it arises, and the pressing necessity of endeavouring to detach the people from it by moral means. These means must be neither puritanical asceticism nor stoical abstinence. You must offer the poor man some substitute for intoxication; you must make other thoughts and other feelings accessible to him; you must not only teach him to read, but must take care that what is worth reading should be within his reach at the lowest possible price. It is true that there is a point at which intellectual culture and morality divide—nay, sometimes appear actually opposed; but in the last and highest development, intellectual and moral culture are similar in kind, are necessary conditions one of the other, and converge into one.

A singing and dancing people is certainly higher in the scale of morality than a sotting people. The national ballad and the national dance open the way to every department of poetry and of music; when people have reached this point it is easy to awaken the feeling for every kind and degree of art. The hundreds who resort to a museum cannot at the same time be sitting in an ale-house or a gin-shop. Nor is this all; they will soon come to feel the boundless disparity that exists between men whom art raises into demi-gods, and animals in human shape degraded by drunkenness below the level of brutes. It is a radical error that Christianity forbids the education of man by the forms, the influences, the conceptions of Art : it forbids only those perversions and misapplications of Art which the noble and the uncorrupted among the Greeks equally rejected.

" Dreams—impracticable dreams !" I hear some exclaim; Art can do nothing ; the catechism and the rod are the only things for educating the people and keeping them in order. In those good old times which some adore, the catechism and the rod were, indeed, the beginning and the end of all attempts to form the social existence of the lower classes. These gave the black and red characters with which priests of a gloomy and distorted Christianity, and nobles of a haughty and igno- rant aristocracy, delighted to stamp the book of social life. But genuine Christianity and true nobility have nothing in common with them; and the world has advanced in these respects, though it may have lost ground in some others.

" All very fine," say many, " but impossible." What is impossible ? Is some little elementary instruction in art, and in judgment of art, im- possible ? Do not, then, thousands and tens of thousands of Prussian children—of Prussian soldiers—learn singing ? And does this mean nothing, or produce nothing but the impressing this or that motion on a certain quantity of air? If the hymns of Luther, and the noblest songs of our poets, are sung by our regiments with more refinement, feeling, and intelligence than the choruses of the ' Messiah' were sung the other night in the most aristocratical concert-room of London, is this no proof of improvement? Is this an impossible vision ? Or should we wish the times back again in which no modest girl dared to pass certain guard-houses for fear of being shocked by obscene songs ? Is it no ad-

vancement in society, no education by the influence of art, that, thanks to Raupach's historical
plays, the greatest emperors, the wisest popes,
the most heroic princes and knights, the noblest
ladies, are now familiar to the very children in
Berlin? whereas, twenty years ago, scarcely any
body, even in cultivated society, knew the names
of the emperors or the kings of the house of
Hohenstaufen, who once bore sway from Lübeck
to Naples?

Is it no improvement that the high and the low
now quit the narrow circle of their daily prosaic
life, and can rejoice and, if I may use the word,
expand, in the company of the most magnanimous
spirits of a time rich in great men and in great
events? That thoughts and feelings hitherto
unknown, nay unsuspected, should now find an
echo in the hearts and heads of the humblest
spectator, and should raise him above himself?
An artistical training and education like this
naturally leads to history, which ought itself to
be a work of art, though differing in its nature
from that of the poet. I venture even to assert
that the questions concerning church, state, faith,
civil obedience, civil liberty—the objects of the
present public and private activity and excitement—would thus be calmed, conciliated, and
purified.

The more sublime and important, however, the
application and diffusion of true and genuine art,
the greater is the danger and the shame when
men of rare talents addict themselves to the false;
when they deface truth and demoralize feeling.

This is the vice (a vice which has not met with half the reprobation it deserves) of the modern French dramatists. While Raupach strives to give to history, truth, feeling, decorum, morality, and religion their just and appropriate province and privilege; while, in his character of poet, he labours to combine all these into one harmony, to surround them with one halo, of art, and, even were he unsuccessful, might justly exclaim " *In magnis voluisse sat est,*" Victor Hugo irreverently tramples historical truth under his feet; transforms one of the greatest of German emperors, one of the profoundest of thinkers, into a shallow fool; a dissolute but gallant king of France into the miserable slave of his passions; a bigoted but chaste queen of England into a profligate woman; and instead of being awed by the dim majestic shadows, before whom even the historian trembles, the soi-disant poet seems to imagine that murder, incest, baseness, and profligacy of every kind are the materials of the highest order of poetry.

He places the hideous and the loathsome on the throne of beauty, and, with curious self-complacency, justifies his folly by distorted quotations from Shakspeare,—the thorough antagonist of all these disgusting perversities and horrors. Shakspeare, even in the most terrible of his characters, leaves a thread of psychological light, which shows the point at which the criminal still holds to the Human, and from which he can yet return, penitent and reconciled, to the Divine. But the writers of this French school make it their business and their delight to thrust the Satanic element into the foreground, and to magnify it under their pretended poetical microscope, till nature and art, virtue and beauty, the Human and the Godlike are wholly lost under the hideous mask.

But whither have I wandered? *quo me rapis?* All I meant to say was, that I went to bed early last night; but it was not so written in the book of fate. At ten o'clock Mr. ——— fetched me; and after we had called two ladies, and driven above half a German mile, we arrived at ———, a musical soirée. The heat in the two rooms was insufferable, and the number of guests so great, that many sat on the stairs and the floor. It cost me immense toil to make my way through this narrow path to the open air ; a longer stay would probably have thrown me, uninitiated as I am, into a fainting fit.

In spite of all the pains I take to understand whatever is strange and unwonted, and to explain it in the fairest manner, I must confess that yesterday I was heated into a temper in which I could not regard parties of this sort as anything better than mere deformities—as a mode to be utterly eschewed and denounced. It is a strange system of tyranny and slavery according to which, with the help of certain strips of paper or card, a man can induce hundreds to hunger and thirst, to toil and sweat, to be pushed and elbowed, to stand instead of sitting, to sigh instead of speaking, and, at the close of all, to return thanks for the honour of the torment.

Nobody will succeed in educating me in any

school of art in this way., What was sung and played was exclusively out of the modern, empty, and pretending school, and therefore deserves to be no further characterized. As I went away several guests were arriving, and W—— received from —— —— the important information, that nobody could possibly appear at the Duke of ——'s before midnight. I thanked God that this cup of fashion was spared me.

Is there nobody at this time of day who, even without Eulenböckh's* wit, could undertake to defend the joyous drinking songs of the lower classes, and turn the laugh against the silly affectations of the higher; who convert night into day, abjure all nature, cheerfulness, ease, comfort, and enjoyment; prohibit all hearty gaiety, and seem to regard the existence of a stewed or pickled herring as the ideal of the life of a fashionable gentleman or lady? Is there not much more sense in the guests of the alehouse, when they untie their neckcloths, and pull off their jackets, and " take their ease in their inn," than in the fashionables, who gasp in their well-tied cravats, or tight stays?

Our forefathers sat round their cups of good wine, and sang jovial choruses; and I should like to know why that was more sinful or tasteless than the complacent dilettante who pipes and flourishes his solo, or the weary auditors who clap their elegantly-gloved hands—so innocently, that one hand knoweth not what the other doeth.

---

* See Tieck's Novelle—Die Gemälde.

When the clockwork has played out its tune, the box is shut up till the next time it is wanted; and so it goes on, without truth, nature, or living feeling, till the tired night-moths vanish with the break of day, fancying the night is gained, and the loss of a day is nothing. All over-refining, all over-seasoning of life punishes itself; and if ever Rousseau's words can be rightly applied, it is in these regions. *Retournons à la nature!*

So much for the sigh extorted from me, for which I deserve to be regarded as for ever incapable and unworthy to hold a place in " a squeeze."

Sunday, June 13*th.*

Numerous and thickly-crowded as the people are in the parties I have just described, they are not really social. The loose thread of a common invitation is by no means sufficient to bind them together. They remain, as in many modern political systems, mere atoms, without form, qualification, or affinity. There must be space to move about, to take a seat, to leave it again, to gather into groups, if personal qualities are to have any meaning or value in society. Without this, who can distinguish the leader or the follower, the speaker or the listener, the grave or the gay, the concerted pieces or the solos of conversation? If all individuality is pressed down to a mere negation, nothing remains but a unison of noise and tumult.

These remarks on domestic society apply equally to the dry and barren ground on which certain politicians seek to found civil society, when they lose sight of the diversity of its materials, and want to cut all to the same pattern and measure. He who, out of the infinite variety of social life, can find but one material to build with —such as the property in a house, the payment of certain taxes, the possession of a certain fortune, the length of residence, or whatever other particularity he may choose to erect into the sole and exclusive rule,—will find that his edifice will not stand.

Here I would break off, but the assent I may perhaps receive from a quarter in which I seldom experience it, causes me to glance at the necessary reverse of what I have just been saying. If these quantitatives—these gentlemen of masses and sums—can see no element of life but in a certain mass, or a certain sum, and reject every consideration of more or less, every variation of matter and form, there are people, on the other hand, who get up *artificial* distinctions, or try to adhere to those which have ceased to exist. Kings and nobles, clergy and laity, rich and poor, landowners and manufacturers, artists and scholars,—all have their place, their sphere of action, their rights; and he who distinctly perceives this given and necessary diversity; he who knows how to measure masses, and to appreciate and utilize peculiar qualities, is the only statesman, in the higher sense of the word. Almost all the schools and parties which divide Europe on these subjects see but one side, and take a part for the whole.

I have wandered a second time into a bye-way, and I am now come to the end of it. I meant to remark, that the atomizing, isolating principle of English parties does not wholly disappear in their meetings for specific objects ; but the necessity and importance of the *corporative* spirit makes itself felt again in an age which had far too hastily declared war upon it. The abuses of close corporations, the monopolies of universities, are so evident, that nobody can deny them ; but it by no means follows that a State consists of one supreme central government, and then of a number of individuals added together, and comprehended under the common term, people. It by no means follows that all large combinations of individuals into one whole inevitably forms a dangerous *imperium in imperio.* On the contrary, every highly civilized state stands in need of great and various organs ; such as associations of artisans, artists, scholars, clergymen ; of cities, towns, rural districts, &c. ; and however times, forms, or objects may change, this corporative spirit, this power of attraction and of reciprocal influence, will always revive like a phœnix from its ashes. The development of the Germanic nations exhibits the edifice of corporate or associated bodies, from the individual up to the empire of the middle ages, in its greatest diversity. Indian and Egyptian castes are a caricature of the divisions into which society naturally falls. The Hebrew tribes relate only to external differences. Patricians and plebeians form an abrupt, irreconcileable, and therefore pernicious contrast; while the Mahommedan world, on the contrary, exhibits a uniformity destructive to all individuality. The German estates, cities, companies, orders of knighthood, guilds, unions, and gradations of the most varied kinds, first realized the idea of a higher and richer political organization; and whatever was defective in former ages, or has become so by the lapse of time, may and ought to be improved and reformed. Not, however, in the French abstract mode of reform, but in the German concrete manner, which seeks to conciliate variety with unity; instead of worshipping the former, like the Italian, or the latter, like the French.

·. There is scarcely an art, or a science,—scarcely anything agreeable, useful, ·or instructive, for which the English have not established special societies, and thus wonderfully increased and strengthened the imperfect means and powers of individual man. The value, the efficiency, the simplicity of such unions, is conspicuous in each and all; especially as individuals in England have more resources at their command than in other countries; while fewer general schemes or important improvements originate with the government. On the one side, therefore, the free will of individuals, their benevolence, activity, and enthusiasm, operate in a most beneficial manner; though, on the other, it is not to be denied that, for certain purposes,—for instance, national education,—one general impulse and one regulating law would correct error and restrain bigotry.

To begin : the clubs here are less instituted for the purpose of eating and drinking together than of reading 'the newspapers. Out of this grow other literary wants, such' as maps, pamphlets, &c., till at last an excellent library is formed, like that at the Athenæum. According to the account which now lies before me, this association has a yearly income of six ·guineas from each member, which, with twenty guineas paid by each on admission, makes a sum total of eight thousand six hundred and ninety-four pounds ; and with this, even in London, something considerable may be effected. Not to mention associations for purely practical ends,— such as insurances, roads, canals, manufactories, and mines,—the Royal Institution affords its members an opportunity of hearing lectures on various sciences. By day, the female part of the audience are the most numerous ; but the weekly evening meetings of the men are in-variably graced by some remarkable and interesting lecture, which produces very different fruits from the attempts of most of our academies, whose speeches few hear, and whose writings few read.

The great associations for hospitals, orphan asylums, &c. occupy the middle place between the purely practical and the purely scientific societies. They are most useful institutions : for example, an hospital at Charing Cross has received about four hundred thousand patients since its foundation.

The London Mechanics' Institute combines

lectures for men, with special instruction for junior classes, and the use of an extensive li-. brary.

A Statistical Society has lately been instituted, with a view of discovering and verifying the statistics of England, in the first place, and then those of other countries : they are arranged under five principal heads, economical, political, medical, moral, and spiritual statistics. By these comprehensive researches, arithmetical statements, which so often deceive, are subjected to a severe examination and correction, before any general conclusions are drawn from them.

The Zoological Gardens, which I have often mentioned before, are also supported by a voluntary association, and now consist of two thousand eight hundred and four members. In the course of the last year, the gardens were visited by 208,583 persons, who paid, for admittance, 7545*l.*; the total receipts amounted to 18,458*l.* Such an income affords ample means of embellishing the gardens, and enriching the collection of animals. The society gave 1050*l.* for a rhinoceros. The garden contains two hundred and ninety-six specimens of mammalia, seven hundred and seventy-six birds, and twenty-one animals of other classes.

But of all the societies (excepting always the Bible Society), that for the Diffusion of Useful Knowledge is undoubtedly the most important. It had its source in the very just notions, that the civilization of the people by means of reading is possible, provided really useful books were writ-

ten for the people; and that these books might
be printed at a very cheap rate, provided the
numbers sold were sufficiently large. Many of
the works published by the society, such as those
on agriculture, and the breeding of cattle, the
almanacs, &c., are remarkably well adapted to
their end; and a vast stock of ideas and of information is circulated in a manner hardly imagined in former times. This is the true means
of destroying a bad and corrupting popular literature. It is curious that so long a time should
have been suffered to elapse since reading was
diffused among the people, before they were provided with anything fit to read. The society has
been reproached with neglecting moral and religious instruction; the answer to this is, that the
diffusion of the Bible and other religious works
is the object of other special associations; and that,
in the actual state of religious parties, it would
be extremely difficult to produce anything which
would not be attacked and decried by one side
or another. Besides, everything cannot be done
at once; and when an interest in literature of
this cheap and intelligible kind is once excited,
moral and religious exhortations will find readier
entrance to the mind, than if they are prema-
turely pressed upon an uncultivated understanding. It is an inestimable gain that interesting
and amusing information concerning the works of
nature, manufactures, arts, eminent men, discoveries, antiquities, &c., should be put before the
people in constant and varied series; that hun-

dreds of thousands who never thought at all, are
led to think on a great variety of subjects.

If our censors were capable of putting forth
a really well-organized and well-written Penny
Magazine, they would do much more for the
purification of our popular literature, than by
placing themselves in a post of avowed danger,
and making so many demonstrations of alarm
and disgust, that everybody perceives that something is the matter, and runs with the greatest
avidity to see what it is.

Sunday, June 14th, 1835.

The day before yesterday I dined with young
M———, who, like his father, has showed me
the greatest attention and civility. I was introduced to Allan Cunningham, the author of ' The
Lives of the Painters.' The conversation turned
on various subjects ; among others, on the system
of the English universities,—so difficult to understand.

Yesterday I dined with Sir R. P. in White-
hall Gardens. His house is enclosed by gardens
on each side, at the back of it flows the Thames,
and on one side there is a beautiful view of Westminster Bridge, on the other of Waterloo Bridge,
over which is seen the great dome of St. Paul's.
The paintings, chiefly of the Flemish school,
which, on account of the candle-light and the
numerous company, I could not conveniently look
at last time, are, without exception, admirably
chosen ; the entire absence of inferior ones

shows the judgment and taste of the collector. Among many, I shall only mention a little landscape by Cuyp,—a castle in a lake,—of a warmth and brightness that I never saw in a Flemish picture. There are such admirable paintings of this master, who is little known in Germany, that I do not hesitate to call him the Flemish Claude.

That taste and splendour were displayed in everything, down to the minutest decorations of the table, may be understood as a matter of course.

LETTER XXXIV.

War of Opinions in England—Contradictory Affirmations on
Agriculture—Prussian Peasantry.

London, June 14th, 1835.

OPINIONS differ in every country, but in none are
they so freely discussed, so fearlessly expressed,
and, in every way, so widely diffused and strenu-
ously attacked, as in England. This has great
advantages; but it is not unattended with its
peculiar difficulties. When the whole current of
opinion and action moves on in one given direction, it is easy to go with the stream, or to suffer
oneself to be borne along by it; but when opposite roads are recommended with equal confidence
as the right, the wanderer, standing in the cross-
ways, either falls into irremediable scepticism,
and loses all belief in truth; or he chooses one
path, and thinks that every body who takes the
other is gone astray—at the least,—or perhaps is
guided by evil intentions. I may add, that an
important question is very rarely agitated *for its
own sake,* in England; the discovery of an objective truth is very rarely a simple, unmixed aim.
Almost everything is blended with personal
motives and political partizanship, in such in-
separable connexion, that an observer has infinite

difficulty in arriving at any clear and perfect psychological analysis.

Ou no subject have I felt this more than on all those connected with agriculture. The most contradictory, incompatible things are asserted with the greatest deliberation, and demonstrated with all the pretension of mathematical truths. Agriculture is making rapid advances; it is going to irrevocable destruction; England can always produce food sufficient for her own consumption; she can never grow enough for her own wants; the corn-laws are 'necessary, superfluous, beneficial, ruinous; the agriculturist is oppressively and unfairly taxed; he is unjustly favoured; the system of leases. is very defective; it is so admirable that no country can exhibit anything equal to it! Such are the things which are daily said, written, and printed; and I am far from having the presumption to imagine I can reconcile these contradictions, or the desire to cut these knots. However, as I have no personal interest in the matter, I will at least endeavour, from my impartial point of view, to introduce some order into this chaos, and, for my own illumination, some light into this darkness. I ought, in true German fashion, to set out with general principles; to advance with logical rigour, and to have one definite point in view; but a travelling German in London is no longer a philosophical pedantic German, and you must accept my letter such as I find it convenient to make it.

Perhaps my observations on the agricultural

state of England will be more just if I first recur
to that of Prussia.   I have a twofold motive for
this, because Professor Jones, in his instructive
work ' On the Distribution of Wealth,' discusses
the condition of our peasantry.   He says that
the new law has transformed the tenant, or dependant holder of land, into a proprietor : but
if he is bound by law to pay a third, or even a
half, of the produce as rent, he is excessively
burthened, and will derive no advantage from the
change; and, in effect, that many have declined
the pretended boon of freedom.   There can be
no improvement in agriculture without capital;
but capital will not be produced under the system
now adopted, and the good effects will probably
not be so rapidly felt as was expected.

Professor Jones's conclusions were correctly
drawn from what he had read or heard—with reference to the point from which he regarded the
subject, and to the end he had in view; but after
I had conversed with him more in detail, we
agreed in all essential particulars, and he was convinced that this affair has very different, and not
less important, aspects.   But as, even in Prussia,
these are sometimes misunderstood and misrepre ·
sented with astonishing pertinacity, it is not superfluous to state in few words what are the means
and ends of our system, and afterwards to compare those of the English and the Irish with them.

If the first idea, to make the new proprietor
pay one-third, or one-half, of the produce as rent,
had been generally adopted, it would have been

in some instances too high, in others too low, and would very rarely have been conformable to the real state of the case. This useless abstract principle was therefore justly abandoned, and only the result of an accurate investigation in every separate case was applied to the several parishes. The general reproach of a too high or too low determination of the payment, therefore, falls to the ground; and whether the individual who pays or receives has, at the first moment, more or less advantage, depends on a great number of subordinate circumstances, chiefly on his property and his judgment. Nor is there any more reason to draw general conclusions from the circumstance, that several of the peasants were not inclined to become proprietors. The cause of their unwillingness was that, in the mode first adopted, regard had been had only to the burthens, which they had hitherto borne, and no due weight given to their rights (for instance, to pecuniary assistance, timber from the lord's estate, &c.) Since the regulations have been amended their disinclination has ceased.

The grant of property in the land, it is added, does not create capital. At first sight, it must be allowed, it rather gives painful evidence of the want of the necessary capital. But it would be most unjust to allege the feeling of the moment as the sole, final, and unsuccessful result of this grand measure. In the first place, every individual is induced, by the new want which he experiences, to look about him with more earnestness and care, for means to provide for it, than under

the old jog-trot system; and these efforts do not
fail to produce fruit. In the second place, the
new proprietors can obtain credit which was
wholly unknown to them in their former circumstances. In the third place, capital increases
with the increase of industry and perseverance.
The peasant, knowing that he labours for himself
and his children, now does more in one day than
he formerly did, as a servant, in the whole week.
It is true that, as a proprietor, he may be more
improvident than he was before, but he will much
oftener think of saving and acquiring; and should
the rent at first appear too high, yet, after a
partial redemption, the second generation will
be more at its ease. Besides, it is a fundamental
error to attempt to prove the excellence of a
state of servitude by the possibility of the abuse
of liberty. If we follow out this course of rea-
soning logically, we come to the system of the
Sudras, the Helots, and negro slaves; and besides,
the abuses which might arise may, and will be,
counteracted by laws on inheritance, acceptance
of the estates, removal of the smaller proprietors, &c.

Lastly, and above all, the conversion of the
Prussian peasants into proprietors was not exclusively undertaken with a view to the increase
of the material produce, but with a moral view,
and for higher objects. If these are attained,
all the rest must follow. And posterity will
confirm, what all real and unprejudiced friends
of their country already know and feel,—that the
legislation of the years 1808 to 1812 awakened

that enthusiasm and energy which led to the overthrow of French tyranny, to intellectual freedom, and to a progress in industry and wealth, such as a narrow policy can never produce. Recent events have afforded fresh and melancholy proof, that a brave and enthusiastic nobility can neither acquire political independence, nor security and improvement of their own possessions, unless supported by a free and enthusiastic people.

If we contemplate the history of the land and of agriculture, we find at first property in the soil in one hand. The proprietor, who is at the same time the occupier, is surrounded only by slaves, who labour for him, and are treated and supported at his discretion. The second form shows us serfs, to whom their master prescribes the quantity and quality of their labour, but at the same time assigns to them a spot of ground, out of the produce of which they may support themselves. In the third period, the undefined services are changed into something definite; and this appears, sometimes as part of the produce (tithes), sometimes in the form of payment in money. Together with a fixed rent in corn or money, there is usually a fixed time for the duration of the occupancy; or the tenant-at-will becomes a leaseholder. The second and third periods show, we cannot say a division of property, but the proprietor,—the receiver of the rent either in kind or in money,—distinct from the actual cultivator of the soil,—the farmer or husbandman. Lastly, the proprietor can either take back the land into his own possession, or sell his claim to the rent; then the proprietor and farmer are the same: which new state of things, however, is essentially different from that in the first period, inasmuch as agriculture is henceforward carried on, not by slaves or serfs, but with the help of free labourers.

I may dispense with an inquiry into the profit of the two methods, because in a moral and philanthropic—that is the highest point of view— slavery and villenage cannot be justified. The inquiry respecting agriculture, as carried on by tenants or by proprietors, is more interesting and instructive. The former is in general the English, the latter the Prussian system. Many writers have commended the former, because, as they allege, the requisite capital is never found until the class of farmers or tenants exists; and agriculture, especially in our day, cannot be carried on without capital. I willingly concede the last half of the position, but I deny the first: for there are poor farmers as well as needy proprietors; and when the latter possess capital, they are as able to make improvements as the former. The main point therefore is, the existence and the application of capital, not the separation of the proprietor from the farmer. Many proprietors, especially of numerous and large estates, are of course unable or unwilling to keep them in their own hands, and the system of letting thus naturally arises; but it by no means follows from this that it is in itself the best

XXXIV.]   AGRICULTURE.   145

system, and the best for both parties, or even for
a whole nation.

Let us begin with the doctrine of the increase of capital, because the panegyrists of the
letting system lay almost exclusive stress upon
it. Will capital be more at the command of the
proprietor or of the farmer? I do not hesitate to
believe the former, for, besides their personal
credit, (which on an average may be the same for
both parties,) the former has the advantage of
the real credit attached to the estate, and is
able in this way to offer security for a mortgage,
which the farmer, as such, does not possess. Hence
so many leaseholders in Prussia endeavour to become fee-farm tenants, and then by redeeming
the rent, to convert themselves into proprietors.
To this must be added, that an attachment to the
soil grows out of secure possession, which the
leaseholder cannot feel; and that his enterprises
are influenced by a thousand considerations which
do not affect the proprietor. If it be said, " Judicious landlords do not inconsiderately change
their tenants, because they know that it is an
advantage to themselves when the tenants feel
security :"—this is saying no more than that
the nearer the situation and condition of the
tenant approaches to that of a proprietor, the
better it is for both parties. But, if we proceed
in this manner, we come to the rule, that the
union of both these characters in one is not the
worst, but the best method.

Should it be objected that "the credit attached
to the estate is but one, and if the tenant has it

VOL. II.   H

not, yet the owner has it; that it is not doubled, because the tenant purchases the estate, or because the proprietor manages it himself;" it may be answered, that in the latter case, the money raised upon credit is regularly employed for the advantage of the land and the improvement of agriculture, which does not happen when proprietors, who let their estates, contract debts.

In our days also many proprietors are induced to manage their estates themselves, because the rent, instead of increasing as they expected, falls off more and more: a circumstance of great importance, and for which a great variety of reasons, most of them unsatisfactory, are assigned.

In the first place, it is attributed to total exhaustion and degeneracy of the soil. There is no doubt that such exhaustion is possible, especially through bad modes of culture, and that it really exists in some instances; but what land, newly brought under cultivation, in poor countries, produces in abundance, is also afforded by old land, where the richer farmer bestows more capital and industry upon it; and so far Europe need not fear any danger of perishing with famine on the worn-out soil. People frequently fall into the error of expecting certain changes and improvements in the modes of culture to produce miracles; which, of course, did not happen. Instead of blaming themselves, they laid the fault on the old ground, because it did not submit to tricks and legerdemain. These and similar results drove many persons, pretending to be judges, into the opposite extreme; they denied that a greater produce would ever be obtained by the employment of greater capital. Thus Ricardo says, " Every greater capital employed in agriculture leads to a decreased rate of production." This cannot possibly be meant as a general assertion, that the production increases with a decrease of capital, or in general, that it is absurd to employ money in agriculture. Perhaps it only means that, if the first 1000*l*. employed on the estate produce 10 per cent., the second 1000 may yield only 8, the third only 6 per cent., &c. At all events Ricardo ought to have expressed himself more clearly, to prevent misunderstanding. But he himself appears not to have had an entirely clear view of the matter, and from too narrow premises, to have been led to ambiguous and unsatisfactory conclusions.

The following is my idea of the matter : in general, the most fertile tracts are first cultivated ; when it gradually becomes necessary to cultivate the more sterile parts, the capital and labour applied do not yield so much profit as at first. When, however, the former lands are sold at a high price, and the latter can be obtained on low terms, the profit, if not entirely, is yet nearly equal. In case, too, with the accumulation of capital, the rate of interest falls, a capital employed in agriculture will not produce so large an income as before. But the same may be said of capital employed in trade and manufactures, though nobody can affirm that the apparent decrease in the amount of profit can never be made good by an increase of quantity ; or that a rich nation, with a lower rate of interest, is worse off than a poor nation with high interest and little capital.

In the second place, much confusion arises on this subject from the want of precision in the terms employed, for instance, the word *rent :* sometimes it was understood to mean the total produce of the soil ; sometimes only the revenue which the proprietor received from the tenant ; sometimes it was required that both should rise and fall in equal proportion; sometimes it was denied that this was, or could be, the rule. Perhaps this complex matter may be made plainer by the following considerations. The ground is no other than the machine with which the cultivator works. He to whom the machine belongs, and who sells or lends it, of course demands either a price or rent for it; if the proprietor, besides the machine, that is the earth, furnishes the means of putting it in motion, for example seed-corn and cattle, this must be brought into account. If he gives, besides, money for improvements, draining marshes, &c., he justly demands suitable interest for this also. By this and similar means, the quantity and quality of the soil being originally equal, he raises his rent in comparison with his neighbour, that is, in case the latter has sold or let only the bare machine. If increase of population and demand make it necessary to bring into cultivation land which has hitherto lain waste, a new rent arises for the proprietor of it; a machine that was unused or despised comes into use, and acquires value. If,

on the other hand, land hitherto cultivated lies
fallow, the machine stands still, and the owner
loses the profit he has hitherto derived from it.
The third case is more complex, when, in consequence of certain changes and improvements,
double the work is performed with the same machine; when, for instance, an acre of land, instead
of six bushels of corn, yields twelve. If the proprietor is also the cultivator, no dispute arises on
this subject; but when they are two distinct
persons, we find opposite opinions and interests;
the former often claims the whole increase, while
the latter will not give up the smallest portion;
and the entire classes of proprietors and tenants
generally join, without examination, in the outcry
of their leaders. The main question, however, is,
to whose capital and skill are the increased produce to be ascribed? Supposing the tenant to
have been the real author of it, the increased advantage is due to him.

But if the effects of the improvement he has
made should extend beyond the term of his lease,
a part of the profit will certainly accrue to the
landlord: only people in general forget that no
tenant will undertake improvements which do not
repay him during the term of his lease, or for
which the proprietor, who subsequently profits by
it, allows him no indemnity. Thus the balance is
preserved,

A machine which performs twice as much as
it performed before, acquires double value; but if
this value only covers the interest of the labour
and capital expended on it, then he who con-

tributed neither labour nor capital has no right, strictly speaking, to demand any thing: if he raises the rent on account of the increased produce, so that the interest of the labour and money expended do not remain over for the tenant, the machine must fall to its ancient value.

On the other hand: if I am able with *one* machine to perform as much as formerly with *two*, one of them (unless the demand should increase) will remain idle. The cultivation of the soil may therefore be extremely improved, the total produce greatly increased, and yet landlord and tenant be in bad circumstances. More of this when I return to the state of things in England.

London, June 15.

In truth, however, I have never lost sight of England; because, without coming to an understanding on certain general principles, we cannot form a correct notion of the state of agriculture, either in England or Germany. I therefore proceed. A monopoly price of corn, or of other agricultural produce, caused by legislation, may raise the income of the landlord; but it must be observed, that this does not happen unless he cultivates the estate himself, or unless his tenant, after the expiration of his lease, agrees to pay a higher rent. He, on the other hand, who buys land after the establishment of the monopoly price, and pays dear for it in consideration of this increase, derives no advantage whatever from that price. Lastly, the income of a proprietor may increase when the competition of

tenants leads to extravagant offers. That this is
of no advantage in the long run, but, on the contrary, leads to the most disastrous consequences,
Ireland affords but too convincing a proof. The
real advantage of the landlord goes hand in hand
with that of the tenant: it is absurd to sepa--
rate and oppose what ought to be united.

. Increasing prices while the expenditure remains the same, says Mr. Jones, increase the
rent of the proprietor. This is true; but only
with the above-mentioned limitations, and so far
as the increased prices are not caused by a diminution of the produce, or by scarcity. For this
state of things does not increase the income either
of the tenant or the landlord: nay, the income may
increase with declining prices—that is, if the quantity of produce (the expense of raising it being the
same) increased in a greater proportion than the
prices declined.

It is an error to attempt to account for the rise
or fall of rent on one ground, without attending to the variety of circumstances which influence it. Among these I reckon, favourable
or unfavourable seasons—increased facility and
rapidity of communication with distant countries
—increase and decrease of the population—of
wages—of the rate of interest—of taxes—of the
circulation of money, &c. The English system
of leases by no means affords a universal remedy against all the sufferings of the landlord
or the tenant. Ou the contrary, they have for
years unanimously made the loudest complaints;
and the reports of the most recent parliamentary

Committee begins (in contradiction to the above-mentioned doctrines) with the declaration, " That the capital of the farmers is far smaller than is usually believed; their trade bad, attended with the greatest uncertainties and the greatest risks." On the other hand, many manufacturers affirm that their interest is sacrificed to that of the farmers, to whom the corn-laws in particular give an unfair advantage.

It is necessary to examine more closely these and similar points. Let us, therefore, first hear those who complain of the state and the decline of agriculture. They affirm, that instead of bringing waste land into cultivation, as formerly, it has become necessary to let much land hitherto cultivated, lie waste, because the produce no longer covers the expenses. For many years the receipts have not been equal to the expenditure, for the former has been extremely diminished by the fall in prices; while rent has been reduced only in some cases, and poor rates, county rates, &c., have increased. Thus the farmer lives chiefly on his capital; and in the same proportion as that diminishes, his credit naturally decreases also; the whole class are sinking into inevitable ruin.

The landowners generally join in these complaints : they say that their rents fall off from year to year, and the value of their landed property declines in the same proportion. No one will any longer employ his money in such an insecure and unprofitable manner. Arable land must be converted into pasture ; England can no longer supply itself with corn by native agricul-

ture; and thus we fall into the hands of self-
interested foreigners, and by injudicious legislation, ruin the noble and useful class of agriculturists;—that theories and predilections in favour
of particular interests would plunge England
into misery from which she never could recover.

Before I state any of the arguments which
have been brought forward in refutation of these
charges, I must say a few words on the history of
the corn-laws; because the one party attributes to
them all the misery, while the other sees in them
the sole safeguard against destruction. Up to the
time of Queen Elizabeth the importation was free,
but no encouragement was given to exportation;
the object being to lower prices for the benefit
of the consumer. In the years 1670 and 1689,
obstacles were thrown in the way of importation,
and bounties granted on exportation—partly to
encourage agriculture, and partly to indemnify
the proprietor for a newly-imposed land-tax.
This first occasioned an artificial state of things.
Immense capitals were invested in agriculture:
the natural result of which, contrary to expectation, was, a gradual sinking in the price of corn,
which continued for a long time. It did not rise
again till the year 1756; the exportation diminished, and the bounty ceased. Between the
years 1688 and 1815, not fewer than seventy-
three different corn-laws were passed, founded
on the most contradictory principles; such as
that all land produces too much, or all too little
corn! How was it possible that such vacillating
measures could have an equable and advan-

tageous influence on agriculture and the corn trade? I can only add a few particulars, by way of illustration of this proceeding.

1. The law of 1770 permits importation and exportation, according to a certain standard of prices.

2. From 1775 to 1790, wheat might be imported for a duty of 6d. on the quarter, if the price was above 48s.

3. From 1790 to 1804, it was fixed that wheat should pay a duty of 2s. 6d. per quarter, if the price was not above 54s.; but that this duty should be reduced to 6d. immediately on its rising above this price. In consequence of temporary circumstances, a bounty was granted on importation in the year 1795; in 1798 the former duty was again laid on; in 1800 a bounty was once more offered upon importation; and at length—

4. In the year 1804, a new general law was passed, by which importation was either permitted, on payment of a duty, or prohibited, according to the state of the prices in twelve maritime districts. If the quarter was at 63s. to 66s., the duty amounted to 2s. 6d.; if higher, it was fixed as low as 6d.

5. In the year 1815, importation was altogether prohibited, so long as the price did not exceed 80s. In some years of scarcity, however, this was not rigorously adhered to.

6. In the year 1828, instead of a fixed duty, a scale of duties was introduced. If the quarter is at 62s., the duty is fixed at 16s. 8d. For every

shilling that the price falls, the duty rises 1s.; for every shilling that the price rises, the duty falls 1s.; and when the price is 73s. and above, the duty is only 1s.

It is evident, that all these laws have arisen out of merely temporary circumstances; the last alone was founded on a general idea—namely, to keep the prices steady, and at a certain height. This object, however, was not attained in its full extent; it rather served to show that other causes, especially productive or unproductive years, have such an immense influence on the prices, that this regulating scale of duties appears quite unimportant and ineffective in the comparison. Much injury was also done by the mistaken notion " that the price at home could not fall below a certain point, on account of the duty: it must be higher, by the amount of that duty, at least, than the price abroad." On this notion the landlords often founded their demands, and tenants their offers; both complain unjustly of the state of agriculture, when they ought rather to attribute it to their own false calculations, and the artificial state of things produced by them.

With this, in my opinion, another great error is connected: this is, that the corn-dealers might now reckon upon stable prices, and England depend on obtaining, in case of need, a sufficient supply from abroad. We, however, see—1. That in late years prices have fallen far more, and the duty risen proportionably higher, than most people expected;—2. That the scale of duties was calculated exclusively on the selling price in England, without any regard to the purchase price. Both are certainly connected, but by no means necessarily in an unchanging proportion. For instance, corn may be so cheap on the continent, in a fruitful year, that England may be inundated with it, in spite of its high import-duty; or, on the contrary, it may be so dear there, that, notwithstanding the reduced duties, not a bushel is imported into England. 3. There have been agreements to purchase, at high nominal prices, in order to raise the market-price, and lower the duty: abuses which could not take place with a fixed duty. 4. Very remarkable consequences are produced by the regulation, that all foreign corn must be bonded; and that it depends on the owner when he shall pay the duty, and what quantity he shall take out of bond, for consumption in the country.

However the consequences of the points here stated or indicated may be understood and explained, the corn trade, which is in itself very precarious, has been rendered doubly dangerous, nay, in part destroyed, by an artificial and fluctuating system of corn-laws. And yet only a free and safe corn trade can properly balance scarcity and abundance to the general advantage. Whatever measure, then, renders the corn trade insecure, must necessarily affect agriculture in the same manner; or how would it be possible, for the sake of a temporary demand from England, to change the system of agriculture on the continent, introduce the growth of wheat, &c. &c. ?

But the prolongation of the dispute about the corn-laws is even more prejudicial to England than to the continent.   No one is able, with any degree of certainty, to calculate upon either an artificial, or a natural state of things ; and the general apprehensions are even greater than the circumstances warrant.   All are unanimous in the assertion, that very many persons are deterred from the purchase of land and from farming, who would otherwise gladly invest their capital in this branch of industry.

What then is it which the two parties demand ? One demands an additional duty on the importation of corn, and a new protecting duty against the importation of wool and cattle ;—the opposite party, on the contrary, insists on the total aboli·tion of the corn-laws.   The former forgets, that no state can in our days act with injustice towards another, without running the risk of retaliation ; and that England would act even more absurdly than Napoleon, by adopting a system of continental exclusion, which would promote, though in a partial and compulsory manner, the independence of the continent on English manufactures.   To this must be added, that at the present moment the price of corn is scarcely lower on the continent than in England ; that the abolition of the corn-laws has, therefore, virtually taken place ; or, at least, that a time has arrived when the abolition will be attended with scarcely any consequences.   There is, besides, such an increasing importation from Canada, and above all from Ireland, that the importation from the continent, and the prohibitions against it, are quite insignificant. Ireland yearly contributes towards the abolition of the corn-laws, which is for the ultimate advantage of the whole empire. In the year 1788, the annual importation from Ireland amounted to no more than 50,000 quarters; in the year 1833, it rose to 572,000 quarters. The average importation of various kinds of corn from Ireland was—

		Quarters.
1825 to 1829	. . .	1,840,000
1829 .. 1832	. . .	2,445,000
1833		2,614,000

And here we must not overlook the fact that wheat is at present of an infinitely superior and heavier kind than formerly. The exportation of oats has of late decreased, in consequence of the more profitable cultivation of wheat. The exportation of bacon and butter from Waterford is greater by one-third than it was twenty years ago, and the exportation of wheat has doubled. The navigation of the Shannon has increased sevenfold, and the communication has been so greatly facilitated by roads, canals, and steam-boats, that distant places are able to assist each other, and prices are more nearly balanced than ever. Including the city dues, embarking and landing, the conveyance by the steam-boats from Dublin to Liverpool costs, for a horse, from £1. 5s. to £1. 10s.; an ox or cow, 11s. to 15s.; a sheep, 1s. 9d. to 2s. 1d., &c. Fresh meat is brought from Dublin to Manchester in eighteen hours.

All this proves how injudicious and impossible it is to cut off English agriculture from the rest of the world. It further results from this—

1. That if agriculture has made such rapid advances in Ireland, it is impossible that the amount of the produce of England, which is so much more favoured, can have at the same time decreased.

2. If the Irish have derived less advantage from it than might have been expected, the main cause is the unhappy system of tenants-at-will, under which the increased produce, for the most part, benefits the lessors alone.

LETTER XXXV.

London, June 16, 1835.

THE opponents of the corn-laws require, in absolute contradiction to the agriculturists, their total
abolition.   Corn, they affirm, is, by those laws,
made, on an average, 20 per cent. dearer, which
imposes a tax of 14,000,000 upon the consumers,
and produces distress among the poor.   The
abolition of the corn-laws would not reduce the
income of the farmers 20 per cent., as is assumed;
because the price of many articles (first of all the
corn which the farmer requires for his own use), as
well as wages and poor-rates, must fall considerably.   A free corn trade is the best means of producing steady prices, and is the only certain guarantee against the greatest of all evils—famine.
Hitherto, say they, the manufacturer has been
exorbitantly taxed, and unless wages are speedily
reduced by the abolition of the corn-laws, English
manufactured goods will be unable to compete
with those of other countries.   England, the capital of the world, cannot be reduced to a dependence
on its own agriculture alone; the most indispensable articles of subsistence ought not to be taxed
like silk or cotton.   The selfish design of raising

the value of landed property, at the expense of all other classes, is now palliated under the pretence that corn-laws are the only means of averting the dangers of a famine, by an artificial increase of the quantity grown at home. That but a few persons were benefited, at the expense of all the rest, by the high price of corn; and it is folly to believe that foreign countries will continue to purchase from England, if their two staple articles of exportation, corn and timber, are obstinately excluded. They will, on the contrary, be compelled to establish manufactures of their own, to consume the surplus produce of their agriculture at home, and their consumption of English goods will diminish from year to year. Besides the corn-laws, there is a long list of protecting duties for the interest of agriculture. Thus, for example, there is a duty on

	£.	s.
Butter, per cwt.	1	11
Bacon „	1	8
Hops „	1	11
Rape and Linseed oil, per ton	39	18
Perry, per tun	22	13
Cider „	21	10
On every Horse	1	0

The importation of oxen, sheep, and pigs is totally prohibited; but there can be no greater mistake than to suppose that importation may be subjected to all kinds of restrictions, without exportation suffering in consequence. If the price of corn rises only five shillings a quarter, from the effects of the corn-laws, a burthen of twelve millions and a half is imposed upon the consumers; whereas the protecting duties granted to manufacturers were absolutely null, in consequence of the natural superiority of the country, in regard to the three main branches of English manufacture;—cotton, wool, and metal.

Permit me to add some detached observations to this statement of the arguments against all corn-laws. Not only the theory of finance and commerce proves that an uninterrupted and unfettered trade between the different nations of the earth is the most natural and advantageous state of things; but the higher principles of morality and religion enjoin these humane and beneficent relations. But if they do not exist—if, especially since the time of Louis XIV., the pernicious system of exclusion, prohibitions of importation, excessive duties, and consequently smuggling, prevail—is not every state obliged, in self-defence, to adopt and to apply the same principles? Will it not be ruined, if, in face of the exclusive and prohibitory system of other countries, it neglects also to exclude and to prohibit? Is it not a folly to attempt, when surrounded by illiberals, to be the only liberal? and will not he who rashly, or for the sake of theoretical fancies, takes the lead in this course fall into poverty and misery, while the more prudent and considerate continue to enjoy a secure gain?

All these questions, without exception, have hitherto been answered in the affirmative, both by theoretical and practical men. But since Prussia (though its geographical figure is unfavourable, though it is surrounded by states which act on the prohibitory system, and, in many other respects, is by no means fortunate), has had the unparalleled courage to adopt, and to apply for some years past, the opposite principles, this great example can no longer be overlooked or ridiculed. On the contrary, it ought to be attentively considered and impartially appreciated. It would then perhaps appear that the doctrine of salutary reprisals, of the necessity of outdoing one another in exclusion, of raising duties till every state attained to the happy isolation of China or Japan—was and is erroneous. By pursuing an opposite course, Prussia, not to speak of innumerable other advantages, has gained, chiefly in two respects. In the first place, by abolishing all corn-laws and laws against smuggling, it has relieved its agriculture and manufactures from an artificial and dangerous situation, and has made a greater return to a healthy state than any other country of Europe. Secondly (while France in particular remained wholly behind,) it placed itself in this respect *à la tête de la civilization;* induced England (as Huskisson himself confessed) to adopt more liberal measures; and, by the force of truth and disinterestedness, brought reluctant Germany to embrace the same views, and to form a union which is in every respect deserving of the highest approbation; and, if all the members of the league pursue a firm and equitable conduct, will produce from year to year more valuable results.

Opposed to this most recent theory and practice, the system of the English corn-laws is wholly
untenable.   But if it is resolved to alter the state
of things that has hitherto existed, it cannot be
done exclusively in one instance, nor in one direction.   Protecting duties for agriculture, and protecting duties for trade and manufactures stand
on the same footing, and what is true of the one
is true of the other.   Difficult and complex as
the calculation is, whether this or that class in
a country is in the long run more heavily burthened, certain facts and results are however
incontestable : for instance, that the duty on
foreign silks was not imposed for the benefit of
the farmers ; that the malt-tax and poor-rates
fall heavier upon them than upon the consumers
or manufacturers, &c.   An abolition of the corn-
laws must therefore be accompanied by a compensation; or the general rule should in future
be adopted, which is essentially the foundation of
the Prussian system ; viz, to impose taxes only
for the purpose of maintaining the public revenue,
not as protecting duties to favour certain branches
of industry, and to extend and force it beyond its
natural limits.   The complaints of the English
farmers and manufacturers neutralize each other
as soon as this common tendency of both is overlooked.   They have only one positive and important result ; namely, that they show more
and more clearly, whether they will or not, the
absurdity of the ancient mercantile system, and
place in a more brilliant light the advantages of
a freer intercourse between nations.

What avails, will many persons object, all these arguments *pro* and *con?* the distress of the farmer and of the landowner is a fact; and can no more be reasoned away than a disease by the idle words of an ignorant physician.   Admitting, therefore, that the distress exists, it however does not exist in England only, but in many of the countries of the continent.   The causes, therefore, cannot be exclusively English—they cannot lie entirely in poor-rates and malt-tax; in the relative situation of the farmer and the manufacturer; in corn-laws, &c. for the farmers and landowners on the continent who complain are little, or not at all, affected by these evils.   Let us therefore say plainly wherein the common error lies, and whence the similar disorder arises.   Not only was a temporary state of things, which forced the produce and the prices to an unnatural height, supposed to be permanent, but people speculated even beyond this height, and bought or rented estates accordingly. And they did not only buy and rent with their own money, but with that of others, borrowed at high interest; and, at the very outset, ordered their household and mode of life (in direct contrast to the ancient simplicity), as if money would never be wanting for all these extravagant expenses.   Here lies the true root of much of the misery, and of the greater part of the complaints. But no legislation can avert the consequences of false speculation; nor ought it to regulate its measures according to the wishes and wants of improvident bankrupts.

But, it is objected, has not the income of the wealthy and prudent landowner declined in the same proportion as that of the poorer and imprudent? Undoubtedly; but in the first place they were not quite free from the common delusion, and raised their rents on the same ground of an unstable state of things. Secondly, this diminution of revenue does not affect only the landlord and farmer, but in a considerable degree all classes of citizens.

As the commercial world has sometimes, as if intoxicated, run into mad speculations, and fancied that rapid gains must continue to rise *ad infinitum*, so the farmers were enticed and deluded by individual indications and occurrences. Thus, for instance, some celebrated agriculturists in England sold a bull for 1000 guineas; sixty-one cows and calves for 7858*l.*, forty-seven cows and calves for 7168*l.*; one hired three rams for 1200*l.*, and seven for 2000 guineas*. An acre of land was let from seven to twelve guineas†, &c. Not a few persons believed in this agricultural gold-mine, and all were well contented with the consequences which resulted from it. On comparing the average of rents from 1781 to 1794, it appears that they had risen one hundred and fifty per cent.; and even now, in these times, so bitterly complained of, they are, in spite of all reductions, ninety per cent. higher than in the years from 1781 to 1794‡. But those who call

* British Husbandry, vol. i.   † Report, p. 278.
‡ Report on Agriculture, quest. 11355.

a reduction of rents of twenty-five or thirty per cent. intolerable, and would most injudiciously make up for this deficiency by an increase of the import duties, should be further reminded, that they now receive these rents in coin, and not, as in former years, in a depreciated paper currency; and that since the prices of so many other things, especially manufactured goods, have very much. declined, they are able to purchase just as much with a smaller sum as they formerly could with a larger.

I now come to the second point indicated above. If all capitals, in whatever manner they may be employed (in manufactures, commerce, the funds, &c.), now return less than formerly; if the rate of interest has everywhere fallen, how can the land-owner require and expect that he alone shall be an exception to the rule? The income produced by the money which he has invested in the purchase or improvement of land decreases like all others; and for this circumstance, this fact, legislation has no compulsory remedy. On the other hand, the landlord enjoys with his fellow-citizens the advantages of accumulated capital and lower interest. He who is willing to see and hear, may find sufficient proofs of all these assertions in the instructive ' Report of the Parliamentary Committee on Agriculture.' He who can give proper security (said Mr. Webb) can borrow money upon land at three and a quarter to four per cent. In the favourable years, from 1808 to 1815, (says Mr. Wright,) people bought

and hired land too dear, and lived on too great
a scale, and they now find it difficult and unpleasant to submit to certain retrenchments. He
who was free from debt, active, acquainted with
his business, and a good manager, is not ruined,
though so much is not gained in a short time as
formerly.

We find the same facts and results in Prussia.
He who purchased large estates with little money,
or took them on lease, and persevered in the old
imperfect system of agriculture, has been irre-
trievably ruined. He who did not venture beyond his ability in his engagements and expenses,
and always adapted his modes of culture to the
existing state of things, has maintained his
ground,—nay, he has gained something. At the
same time an important consequence ensued from
the distress of the former. It appeared that the
landowner must be a farmer, as much as the
owner of a manufactory is a manufacturer. It is
only when the profit, which becomes insufficient
by being divided between landlord and tenant,
comes into one hand, that chief of the distress
complained of vanishes. Nobody thinks of buying
a sugar manufactory, a ribbon or silk manufactory, if he has no acquaintance whatever with
those trades; he does not suppose that he can let
it to advantage, and that the manufacturer, besides ample profit to himself, can pay a high rent.
And why should it be otherwise with agriculture?
The times are past when a wholly ignorant person might carry it on with advantage, or manage

large farms.   The person and capital are of more
importance than ever.   But, as we have seen, the
land-owner who farms his own estate, can raise
capital more easily than the tenant, and agriculture was, and must remain, a noble employment.

If, however, the farming of large estates by the
owner (capital, knowledge, and activity being
equal) is to be preferred to the farming by a
tenant, and if the former more easily bears acci-
dents and unfavourable temporary circumstances
than the latter, this is far more the case with
smaller estates.

Even the larger English farmers (it is alleged
by many witnesses) by no means avail themselves of the discoveries of theorists and the
experience of practical men, to the same extent
as manufacturers do.   The former live more
isolated, read and hear much less than is supposed, have their predilections and their habits;
whereas the latter are compelled to adopt without delay every improvement, or run the risk of
being outstripped and driven from the market.

The fluctuation and sinking of prices has, in
latter times, induced many farmers rather to pay
a corn-rent than a money-rent.   This expedient
or remedy appears, however, to be insufficient:
for, 1st. The average prices of former years prove
little or nothing for succeeding years.   2nd. The
payment in kind, or according to the prices of
the last current year, is, in cases of bad crops, the
most oppressive of all.   3rd. It is an inaccurate
mode, while the kinds of cultivation are so dif-

ferent, to pay the whole rent in corn, or to calculate it on the price of corn. Consequently it
would be necessary to fix a maximum and a
minimum for very abundant and for very unproductive harvests, or to have regard to the whole
quantity of corn reaped, and to the market prices;
and thus we again approach a mean price which
is best expressed in money.

In the north of England, and in Scotland, the
farmer usually obtains the land without being
bound to pay for, or take, the stock. This mode
is highly commended, among others, by Messrs.
Kennedy and Grainger, in their work on 'The
present State of Tenancy of Land in Great Britain,' because a farmer of small property may
venture on a greater undertaking, keeps his
capital together for improvements, and does not
exhaust his means on taking possession. This
mode, the liberty of purchasing the cattle, farming utensils, &c., anywhere, and in any manner, or
of bringing them with him, may have its advantages, but it appears to me that the proof is not
complete. For if the stock necessary for the
business of the farm belongs to the landlord, he
can of course demand a higher rent than if he
lets only the bare ground and the empty barns
and outhouses. If the tenant who goes away is
not paid for any improvements, he will endeavour
not to leave any behind him. If the new comer
must purchase or bring all with him, the same
capital is invested in these things, and the only
question is, whether it is more convenient and
advantageous, or more inconvenient and preju-

dicial, to receive them from the farmer who removes, at an appraisement, or at a price mutually agreed upon. All stock has its value in money, and he who parts with it must reckon upon the interest of the capital invested in it, and obtain it by some means or other.

June 17th.

Though all I have meant to say, or said, in the preceding account is, if not circumstantially detailed, yet touched upon, permit me, in conclusion, to put together some few thoughts and opinions under different heads.

1.—The corn-laws are at this moment, when the prices on the Continent and in Great Britain are almost equal, a dead letter, and the present time ought not to be allowed to pass over without making an approach to a natural state of things, before the whole system is violently overthrown in a year of scarcity.

2.—No scale of duties, no importation, regulates the prices in the country; but above, all, the abundance or deficiency of the harvest. For instance, there were imported

Years.	Quarters.	At the average Duty of		
		£.	s.	d.
1829	1,268,000	0	9	4
1830	1,494,000	0	6	7
1831	1,088,000	0	4	9
1832	162,000	1	3	9*

* Hansard, xvii. 753.

According to Jacob's estimate, the harvest produced

In 1820	.	16,000,000	quarters
1824	.	11,500,000	„
1825	.	12,700,000	‚‚
1826	.	13,000,000	„
1827	.	12,530,000	„

The total import amounted from 1816 to 1828 to 6,780,000 quarters; therefore on an average for one year 565,000, or about one-twentieth of the consumption.

3.—The question, whether England is able to supply itself with corn, evidently depends on the abundance of the harvest and the progress of agriculture; but not less on the rearing of cattle, and the constantly increasing consumption of potatoes. High duties do not produce great crops, nor do low duties necessarily lead to the decline of national agriculture.

4.—The greater freedom and equality with which the corn trade is carried on, the more easily will England be able to draw upon foreign countries for the supplies of which she has need.

5.—The distress of the farmers and land-owners is not a general, unmitigated, deadly evil: it is merely a crisis, which may and will be succeeded by a natural, healthy state. The vast majority of the important class of the day-labourers is not affected by this crisis, unless the seeds of disease are introduced among them by a false application of the poor-laws.

6.—In the reign of Queen Anne, 1439 acres of common land were enclosed; under George I. 17,000; under George II., 318,000; under

George III., 2,804,000. Between 1811 and 1831 the number of agricultural families in England were augmented by 64,000; those employed in trade and manufactures 159,000; the number of inhabitants in Great Britain 4,000,000. The importation of provisions has not risen in the same proportion as the consumption. Hence it incontrovertibly follows that, whatever may be the condition and the profits of the tenant and landlord, yet

a. — The price of that indispensable article corn can never fall for a long period below the cost of production; not even when, as in Prussia, importation from abroad is permitted and facilitated.

b. —English agriculture, with comparatively the smallest number of hands, produces the largest crops, and supports by far the greatest number of individuals not agriculturists. But if the number of agriculturists is comparatively smaller, and the quantity produced greater than in other places, the capitals must be larger, the mode of cultivation better; knowledge of the business more general; the facilities (for instance, good roads, canals, navigation, &c.) more numerous; it necessarily follows, in a word, that English agriculture, if we take a general view, must be on the whole flourishing, progressive, and more perfect than in any other country in the world. And of this I am thoroughly persuaded; notwithtanding all the lamentations which distress here and there extorts, or which party spirit has often put forward to serve its own ends, but which will hardly serve its turn much longer.

LETTER XXXVI.

Manufactures—Comparison of ancient Times with modern—Relations of Master, Journeyman, and Apprentice, in the Middle
Ages—Guilds—Causes of their Decline—Advantages of the
old System—Law of Master and Apprentice—Factory Children—Factory Bill—Condition of Workmen—Machinery—
Comparative Production of England—Steam and Human
Labour.

THE materials for my letters have been so abundant, that I have not been able to touch upon
some most important subjects. I have been in
part withheld from doing so until, by reading
and conversation, I had enlarged my information
and removed some of my various doubts. This
has not yet been completely accomplished; nevertheless I shall give free course to my pen and
my thoughts, in the hope that I may be enabled
hereafter to correct whatever errors, and fill up
whatever chasms, my present imperfect knowledge
may occasion.

The subjects I am now going to touch upon
(to treat were saying far too much), namely,
manufactures, trade, finance, the taxes, and the
public debt, are of such immeasurable extent,
and so intimately connected, that I have more
need than ever to bespeak your indulgence in
behalf of the want of arrangement, the omissions, and the repetitions which you will doubtless
find.

If we begin with manufactures, we shall be struck with the infinite difference between former times and present, both as to persons and things. You know that I have frequently entered the lists against the absolute contemners of ancient institutions. I advert to them again here, because the advantages or disadvantages of the present can be clearly discerned only on a comparison with the past. In the middle ages, we find the persons engaged in manufactures in a three-fold gradation: master, journeyman, and apprentice. We find also the connexion of the former with the main body, of which his vocation constituted him a member,— the guild. In what, let us ask, consisted the advantages of this order of things ?

First,—The goodness of the manufactured article,—the product,—was guaranteed by the time devoted to learning the craft; by preliminary examination and probation, and by the testimony of competent persons. It was an obligation, sanctioned both by law and by honour, to reject all incompetent candidates.

Secondly,—The instruction in the trade or craft was connected with domestication *in* the family, and the education of the apprentice *by* the family. Between master, journeyman, and apprentice there existed, not only a material, but a moral connexion, often drawn closer by the ties of marriage.

Thirdly,—The variations in the state and relations of commerce and of prices were comparatively slight; they seldom went to ruin, or even greatly to impoverish the manufacturer. The alternations of hope and fear were proportionally slight. The small number of dependants of the master,—a few journeymen and apprentices, —easily found means to adapt themselves to, or to overcome, the altered circumstances.

Fourth,—The guild was not merely an association for the purposes of trade; it had also a military and a political or civic character and importance. By the guild, men passed from the mere atomistic system, which recognizes only individuals, as such, in the state, into an association actuated by a common thought, and tending to a common purpose. Out of the idea of all these organs, which exercised a mutual restraint and influence on each other, arose that of the Community; and hence we arrive at the State,—an idea with which, I must repeat, the much-lauded atomistic tendency of some modern political doctrines is often at direct variance.

I assume that you will not contest this favourable view of ancient institutions, which is borne out by history; and shall proceed to the question,— What is the cause of their decline and disappearance? Answer—First, as soon as the guilds became close,—as soon as, from sordid and selfish motives, they threw obstacles in the way of new members, and obtained an abusive monopoly and command over prices,—the guarantee for the goodness of their wares lost all meaning and value. The incompetent often ruled in the guild, and the most skilful found it difficult, if not impossible, to gain a livelihood. In the second place, many trades demand a combination of more hands and more implements. than are at the command of an ordinary master, and these gradually grew. into what we now call manufacturers.

Connected with this was, Thirdly, the formation of large capitals, by means of combination; and hence, the impossibility for the poor to compete with the rich.

Fourthly,—The development of individuals and of nations took such a turn, that the collective idea of a guild, and the collective idea of the sum of them no longer afforded a convenient element of political institutions. Just as little was the city-guard, or militia, adapted for carrying on war on a large scale, or according to modern tactics. In short, a multitude of causes rendered it as impossible to retain the old state of things unaltered, as it would now be to restore it. I must, however, maintain, that some portions of the old institutions might be usefully adopted in conjunction with the new; that, indeed, spite of the astonishing results of the modern system, some advantages are lost, which have not been, which perhaps never can be, repaired.

These appear to me to consist in the simple and genuine humanity which marked the relations of the different classes of society. The mildest, the kindest proprietor of a great manufactory cannot possibly organize anything like a domestic life in common with his numerous workmen. He is so far removed from them, that any intellectual or moral community, or mutual influence—any immediate or personal education—is

out of the question.   Thus the democratic mass
of the workmen. stand apart, neglected, or inso-
lent : the relation of master to man has vanished,
or is totally altered.   Least of all can the daughters of the lords of manufactories act as a bond
of union in that domestic life which formerly grew
out of the life of the artisan.   Children indeed
there are, and in countless numbers; the reflections which their appearance suggests are but too
obvious.   The manufacturer excels any master of
old times in wealth and magnificence; whether
he surpasses him in that security and serenity of
existence which arose from the moderation of his
gains and his expenditure may be questioned.

Who then, we may inquire, has gained by all
the changes which modern times have produced,
if not the manufacturer and his workman?   Perhaps those for whom they work—the buyer, the
public.   And if buyers are, in another point
of view, sellers, the gain must be distributed
over all.

I pass on from this suggestive preface, to details, and begin again with persons.   In early
times, apprentices were usually taken by masters
on a special agreement, in which it was set down
what was to be given, and what required in
return.   If there were lawful grounds for the
apprentice quitting his master before the expiration of his term, the latter was obliged to return
a portion of the premium (determined by a
magistrate).   If the apprentice left his master
without reason, he was bound to make him compensation.   The master might keep his appren-

tice in order; but if he or his wife beat him, this was held to be sufficient ground for putting an end to the contract. If, on the other hand, the apprentice struck his master or mistress, he was imprisoned for a year.

Many humane persons have maintained, that the children who work in factories are in a far worse condition than apprentices were formerly, or even than negro slaves. These children, say their advocates, though but from nine to fourteen years old, work from ten to sixteen hours a-day; and, when they are discharged, exhausted with toil, hurry to the gin-shop; suffocating heat and dust, constrained and uneasy postures, double the burthen of this excessive and protracted labour, and destroy their health.

Instruction and education are out of the question; and the Sunday-schools, to which the weary children are taken on the only day on which they could enjoy bodily relaxation, are but a miserable substitute for a real education. I need not say that philanthropists and parents were found, in great numbers, who desired an amelioration of the condition of these poor children; and on the 27th of June, 1832, Lord Morpeth presented a petition on the subject, which measured 2322 feet in length*.

On these complaints were founded proposals for shortening the period of work, making it obligatory to send children to school, &c.

On the other hand, it was said that things of

---

* Hansard, iii. 1055.

this nature can neither be regulated nor removed by legislation;—that the employment of the children was by no.means so laborious and painful as it had been described, but (since the machines executed by far the hardest parts) generally of a kind requiring no great exertion;—that they were as healthy, on an average, as other children, and the operative manufacturer as long-lived as the husbandman. If the time of labour were reduced, the wages must of course be reduced, or the price of the manufactured article be raised in proportion. But as the latter is impossible, on account of the competition of other countries, the former must of necessity be resorted to; in which case the condition of the workman will be rendered infinitely worse by this pretended relief.

And so it has turned out. The ' Factory Bill,' for regulating the hours of wages, providing for sending the children to school, &c., has remained, in great measure, a dead letter; and the masters and workmen of manufactories form such arrangements with each other as they will or can.

The complaints concerning the condition of the factory children are far from embracing all the difficulties of the case: it is affirmed that the wages of the adult workmen are generally so depressed, that they cannot subsist upon them, and are thus driven to illegal measures (such as combinations for raising wages).

To this it is replied, that it is not the depression of wages, but the mode of living of the workmen, which causes their misery, and that those who receive the highest wages are generally the most dissolute. The assertion that the condition of the labourer depends entirely on his earnings is false and mischievous; it depends quite as much on his expenditure. If, instead of the three shillings he received a few years ago, he now receives two, and with these two can buy more bread, beer, meat, and manufactured goods than before with the three, his condition is, in fact, improved. That this is actually the case may be proved by accurate calculations, and may also be inferred from the general appearance of the workmen, from the large deposits in the savings-banks, and from many other facts. The trades' unions, from which many apprehended the entire dissolution of social order, have almost disappeared; they have, at least, become quite insignificant since the over-rigorous laws against combination were repealed, the causes of artificial excitement thus removed, and those who sought a cheap martyrdom, and a base celebrity, thrown back into their original obscurity.

It would, however, be absurd to deny that poverty and mistaken notions are still to be found. They chiefly arise—

First,—From the want, already mentioned, of a stricter community of interest, and a better understanding between manufacturers and their workmen. What can no longer be effected by domestic influence must be done, as far as possible—very inadequately it must be—by school education.

Secondly,—Workmen who are only competent to execute the simplest processes cannot possibly have more than the smallest wages: they expect, however, to live as well as the skilled and consequently highly-paid workman,—though they sometimes refuse to learn anything new, or to take any pains to improve in their own department.

Thirdly,—The introduction of machinery has, for the moment, thrown many workmen out of their accustomed employment; prudence and justice, therefore, equally demand that the legislature and the manufacturers should do everything in their power to facilitate the transfer of their labour into new channels. Thus, for instance, the " hand-loom weavers" have suffered severely of late years,—though no machine can effect exactly what gives its peculiar superiority to hand-weaving.

The hatred of machinery is daily on the decline. Popular writings have tended to enlighten the lower classes, and works like that of Mr. Babbage the higher, on the true bearings of this question. How times are altered in this respect! You and I well remember that the opinion expressed by Rector Snethlage, in a long treatise on the subject—that all machines should be destroyed, and only little models preserved in cabinets and museums, as proofs of the power of human intellect and skill—that this nonsense, actually passed with many for wisdom and humanity. It is not more certain that two and two make four, than that since the invention, and by means of the employment, of machinery, more people can be, and actually are, employed than before. He who doubts this should read the works I have alluded to above. Two examples are all I can find room for here.

In the middle of the last century, the annual consumption of cotton goods in England amounted to twelve millions of yards: it now amounts to four hundred millions. This article, therefore, which contributes so materially to the health, comfort, cleanliness, and innocent pleasure of the lower classes, has been increased in a ratio infinitely greater than the population. A far greater number of workmen are employed than before, while every individual in the country participates in the advantages. What perhaps 350,000 people now produce, would have required 42,000,000 hands half a century ago: that is to say, one man now accomplishes as much as a hundred and fifty did at that period.

According to a calculation now before me, one workman now produces as much as two hundred and sixty-six in former times; or 252,297 persons employed in the cotton manufactories of a large district of England now produce as much as would formerly have required 67,000,000 of hands. And this wondrous augmentation of human power and human dominion over matter ought to be destroyed, or denounced as a calamity! A century ago the use of stockings was confined to comparatively few; now 50,000 families are employed in the manufacture of them; and the export amounts to 1,200,000*l.*—*i.e.*, to as much as the value of the whole cotton manufactory in 1760.

With the consumption of one bushel of coals, which costs threepence, or a fourth of a shilling, a steam-engine raises as much water as could be raised by human labour for fifty shillings. If the coals employed in England, in the various operations of manufactures and commerce, were replaced by human hands, the whole agricultural population would be required to execute the same quantity of work. But the profits of their labour would not nearly suffice for their subsistence—not even were coals twenty times as dear as they now are: the inevitable effects of which would be to annihilate all those manufactures which are calculated upon cheap fuel.

LETTER XXXVII.

Systems of Trade—Truck System—Wages—Iron—Coals—Silk —Wool—Cotton—State of Manufactures and Manufacturers in England.

London, June 16, 1835.

I HAVE directed your attention to the different modes of carrying on trades and manufactures in the middle ages and in modern times. Of the existence and importance of this difference no one can doubt. But it is not universal—it applies only to some of the larger manufactures, while many hand-labours are carried on in the old system, or in modes nearly akin to it. This may be seen from the following list of some of the most numerous trades. There are in England—

13,884	Ship-builders.
18,859	Carters, and drivers of various vehicles.
19,000	Millers.
22,000	Grocers.
28,000	Bakers.
35,000	Butchers.
49,000	Masons.
58,000	Smiths.
74,000	Tailors.
133,000	Shoemakers, &c.

The greater number of trades carried on by masters, journeymen, and apprentices, still afford some of the advantages I mentioned in my former letter, while they have gotten rid of many abuses which had crept in.   But to want to crowd manufactories of silk, cotton, &c. into the space of ordinary rooms, is to push the love for the old system to folly.   They have all taken their natural direction, and have changed, or remained unchanged, as the nature of things required.

Before I give you some details on certain branches of manufacture, I must mention the so-called ' truck system.'   It consists mainly in this,—that the master-manufacturers pay their workmen, not in money, but in commodities.   The opponents of this system, in and out of Parliament, maintained that its certain tendency was indirectly to depreciate wages, and that chiefly for the advantage of the master.   When a man receives money, he knows what he has; when he receives goods, he has to consider not only the quantity, but the quality, which is so difficult to determine.   The prudent workman can lay by money, but he can save nothing out of the bad butter and rank cheese which he is forced to take at high prices, under pain of being turned off*.

To this it was replied, that it was a mistake to suppose that the conditions relating to wages could be determined at the will of the masters. They depend on a hundred things, more especially on. demand and on prices.   No legislation can ensure that labour shall be exclusively paid in money ; and the contrary system has often been attended with the best effects : for instance,

* Hansard, i. 1043; iv. 924; viii. 9.

among the Scotch agricultural labourers. When a master provides that his workmen should find all the articles of which they have the most constant need, in their immediate neighbourhood, and at reasonable prices, this is a great advantage to them, for he is generally satisfied with smaller profits than the little grocer or dealer. There is no question of throwing masses of goods of their own manufacture upon the hands of the workmen to sell again : this would be impracticable; the only thing attempted is, by introducing a system of payment in the most necessary articles of consumption, to lessen the amount of the metallic circulation. The prevailing evils, it was added, were no more the consequences of the truck system, than they formerly were of the price of provisions, or of the forestalling and regrating, so long the object of popular and legal persecution. But granting that the truck system involved a depreciation of wages—this depreciation cannot be prevented when the producing causes exist; and if the truck system were prohibited, the master manufacturers would then be compelled to pay lower money wages. If the causes of any change unfavourable to the workman are not in operation, he leaves the master who underpays him, and seeks better wages elsewhere.

Experience has shown that no general laws can regulate or prevent private contracts of this kind. People pay after, as they did before, in money, or in orders for commodities; and the receivers find themselves equally well, or equally ill, off under both systems; and are either able to make better terms, or are compelled to submit to the resistless force .of circumstances. That these, however, are by no means worse, generally, than in former times, may, as I have said, be distinctly. proved; and individual cases of poverty cannot· possibly be removed or remedied by general laws regulating wages.

I give a few details on particular manufactures.

1. *Iron.*—For a time the price of iron wares sank, because the demand was not quite equal to the supply. The weekly wages of a workman, however, still amounted to from 24*s.* to 30*s.* In the· year 1780, 70,000 tons were smelted; in the year 1831, 750,000 tons; that is, twice as much as in all the rest of the world. From this arises such an universal, convenient, and profitable applica- tion of iron to a thousand different purposes, as no country—and least of all France, with its system of monopoly—can have an idea of.

2. *Coals.*—In the year 1780 the demand for coals amounted to $2\frac{1}{2}$ millions of tons per year; in the.year 1833 to 18 millions. The increase of· population (according to Bowring) has been during that period 90 per cent., the increase in the demand for coals 730 per cent.; and it is calculated that there is no fear of a falling-off in the supply for 2000 years.

3. *Silk.*—In the year 1820 Mr. Huskisson said, " It is to be ascribed to the prohibitive system, that we have remained so far behind our neighbours in the manufacture of silk." When, however, the prohibition was removed, and foreign silks were

admitted on payment of a duty of 30 per cent. on the value, an universal clamour arose, that this branch of trade was declining *. The restoration of the old law was demanded by the silk-weavers of Spitalfields with the greatest vehemence. The very proper answer given was, that the prohibition on the importation of silks would raise the prices only, and not the rate of wages; and that laws were not to be passed for the exclusive advantage of one class. That the distress of which they complained arose partly from the circumstance that the number of silk-weavers had greatly increased; but still more from the establishment of manufactories in districts in which the authorities did not interfere to regulate the rate of wages; and that active and intelligent manufacturers took the place of indolent and negligent ones. It was also proved that the competition consequent on the introduction of French silks had so much improved the English ones, that the best of those of former times would now find no sale. In the year 1823, English silks to the value of 140,000l. only were exported; in the year 1830, to the value of 437,000l. The demand and importation of raw and spun silk, in 1823, amounted to 2,430,000l.; in 1830, to 4,693,000l. So little were the predictions of the enemies of free trade fulfilled. Even the duty of 30 per cent. is too high, and ought to be lowered.

4. *Wool.*—From 1660 to 1825 the export of wool was prohibited; and the import, since 1802,

* Hansard, xiv. 1190.

burthened with more or less duty.   Thus on the
cwt. it·was

	s.	d.
In the year 1802 .	5	3
From 1813 to 1819 . .	7	11
From Oct. 1819 to Sept. 1824 .	0	6

on the pound, in consequence of Mr. Vansittart's
ill-judged advance; from September to December
1824, 3d.

Since the 10th of December, 1824, if the
pound is worth more than a shilling, one penny ;
if worth less, a halfpenny.

Altogether there have been imported in the

Years.	lbs.
1820 . . .	9,700,000
1821 . . .	16,600,000
1822 . . .	19,000,000
1823 . . .	19,300,000
1824 . . .	22,500,000
1825 . . .	43,700,000
1826 . . .	15,900,000
1827 . . .	29,100,000

Besides these facts, which I have extracted from
the 'Report on Manufactures.*,' there are the
following tables in the 58th volume of the 'Edinburgh Review.'

Years.	Millions of Pounds.	Years.	Millions of Pounds.
1820 .	7	1826 .	17
1821 .	15	1827 .	27
1822 .	16	1828 .	31
1823 .	18	1829 .	22
1824 .	23	1830 .	31
1825 .	41	1831 .	29

* Page 79.

There is, then, a very great fluctuation, which perhaps may be partly, though certainly not altogether, accounted for by the duties. Imprudent speculations have met with too severe punishment in this branch of trade, and they have been more common in Germany than in any other country. The importation from thence, for instance, according to a report, was in the years

1820	.	.	5,113,000 pounds.
1825	.	.	28,799,000 „
1826	.	.	10,545,000 „
1830	.	.	26,073,000 „

Notwithstanding the gradually increasing importation, and the decreasing import duty, the prices of English wools have advanced, and the quality of English cloth has improved—a fresh proof of the defectiveness and error of the old theory and practice. The principal ports are London, Hull and Poole. The influence which a good or bad breed of sheep has on the price of the wool is strikingly proved by the difference in the price of a pound of Russian wool and a pound of Saxon; the former of which costs, on an average sixpence, the latter six shillings, or twelve times as much.

It appears, however, very probable that the favours of nature will more than counterbalance all the exertions of art.

The Australian wool is the longest and finest, and the best for spinning. The price of it has risen from 1s. 3d. to 1s. 10d. and even 2s. 10d. a pound. The freightage from New South Wales to England has likewise decreased from 2½d. to

$1\frac{1}{2}d.$ per lb., and the ship-owner has, notwithstanding, a greater profit, because formerly he
was obliged to take in ballast, which yielded him
nothing. In the year 1822, New South Wales
exported 172,880 lbs. of wool, and in 1829
1,005,883 lbs.*; in 1830, 1,967,000, or 300,000lbs.
more than the whole of Spain. As Ireland is
become a powerful rival to Germany in the production of corn, so is Australia in that of wool.
It is, however, impossible to predict anything as
to the future, from these numbers, since no one
knows to what extent home consumption and the
British demand may, and in all probability will,
increase.

5. *Cotton.*—No branch of manufacture has
made such inconceivable progress in modern
times as cotton weaving. This has not arisen
from any protection of government, or from the
uncertain and capricious acts of legislation, but
from the nature of things, and the inventiveness
and activity of manufacturers. Cotton is cheaper
to produce and easier to manufacture than flax,
and has always, therefore, been, for some purposes, preferred. In the year

1787 .	.	. 4,000,000 lbs. were spun.	
1805 .	.	19,000,000	..
1812 .	.	61,000,000	
1820 .	.	137,000,000	„
1826 .	.	162,000,000	
1832 .	.	273,000,000	„

The value of cotton goods amounted, in the
year 1769, to about £200,000, now (official value)

* Hansard, xiii. 1090.

to 40,000,000. I borrow what follows from Baines's excellent 'History of the Cotton Manufacture :'—In the year 1833, 237,000,000 lbs. were imported into England from North America :

	lbs.
From Brazil	28,000,000
From Turkey and Egypt . .	987,000
From other countries . . .	1,696,000
From the English colonies . .	35,000,000
North America exported, in 1701,	189,000
„ „ 1832,	322,000,000

The price of a pound of cotton wool varies from 4d. to 1s. 8d.; but has fallen considerably (like many other things) since 1816. The principal port for its importation is Liverpool. In the year 1833, 840,000 bales were exported from thence, and only 40,000 from London, and 48,000 from Glasgow.

The duty on the importation of foreign cotton goods rose gradually to 75 per cent.; Mr. Huskisson lowered it to 10 per cent., and yet the importation, instead of increasing, as many feared it would, has diminished. In 1826, the value of the cottons imported was £710,000; in 1831 only £35,000—a sufficient proof, were there no other, that duties might be entirely taken off.

There are now 1154 cotton mills existing in England. Water-power, to the amount of 10,000 horses, and steam-power to that of 30,000, are employed in them: 220,000 persons are directly, and one million and a half are indirectly, engaged

in them.   The seven counties in which the cotton
manufactories are the most flourishing, in the
year 1753 contained only 791,000 inhabitants;
in 1831, 2,753,000.   There were exported to

	Plain cotton goods.	Coloured goods.
Russia	2,750,000	272,000
Germany	16,527,000	34,951,090
Italy	34,000,000	13,000,000
Brazil	36,000,000	23,000,000
Turkey	15,000,000	3,000,000
China and East Indies	35,000,000	16,000,000
North America . .	13,000,000	18,000,000

In spite of this immense increase, one often
hears it asserted on the Continent, that the English manufactures are falling off; the workmen
starving; the manufacturers obliged to sell under
prime cost, and on the brink of ruin.   These
complaints, which have, from time to time, been
made in England, and those of the farmers,
which were still more clamorous, induced Parliament to appoint select committees, on which the
best-informed persons of all classes were appointed.   Prejudices and errors enough, of all
kinds, were displayed; but, on the whole, sound
and clear notions have made amazing progress,
in consequence of this admirable proceeding.
The Report on Manufactures contains 12,000,
that on Agriculture 12,903, questions and answers; and these have produced a strong and
beneficial effect on the public mind.
   In the former inquiry it is far more evident

than in that concerning agriculture, that the embarrassments or the sufferings affected only certain particular points of time and place, but that on the whole the manufactures were in a very thriving condition! I shall return to this subject, in treating of commerce, and shall only make one observation, by way of guarding against misunderstandings.

It is unquestionable that a manufacturer may, at particular moments, be compelled to sell a commodity cheaper than he can produce it ; he may prefer this loss to giving up his business, or to suffering his stock to accumulate ; but it is folly to imagine that any man, or class of men, will continue to sell under prime cost. People reply, the masses of goods exported from England increase, while their value diminishes ; this is a plain proof that the manufacturers sell at a loss, merely for the sake of ruining the foreign competitor. Not to mention that this preposterous course is open to every man who likes to try it, the fact abovementioned may be explained on very simple grounds.

In the first place, wages fell nominally and really, because cash payments were resumed instead of payments in paper. But as corn, clothing, and other articles fell yet more in proportion, the workman is, as I have already remarked, better off, on the whole, than before. Wages now vary from 2s. a-week for the youngest child employed to as high as 35s.

In the second place, the manufacturer does not make so large a profit on his capital as before ;

but as capitals are generally increased in a greater ratio than profits and interest have fallen, he is at least as well off as formerly.

Thirdly, cotton-wool has fallen in price, and a multitude of new inventions have so much facilitated manufacture, that a much greater bulk of goods can now be sold for the same money, and yield the same, or indeed greater, profit. The yarn, or twist, costs on an average about half as much as in the year 1815; such, indeed, is the rapid progress of machinery, that twist, for instance (No. 100), which, in the year 1786, cost 1*l.* 18*s.*, was sold in the year 1832 for 2*s.* 11*d.*

From all this it conclusively appears how foolish it would be to attempt to fix the rate of wages by law, or to hold to the prohibitive system, or to tax machinery in order to perpetuate the existence of old implements. Free development will be sure to find the right channel, if artificial impediments are not thrown in its way.

Whether, however, the commercial situation of the world be pregnant with more danger or more advantage to England, is a question we shall be better able to answer when I have put together a few facts concerning commerce.

LETTER XXXVIII.

State of Commerce and Manufactures in England—Glove-trade
—Decline of Monopolies—Navigation Laws—Prussian Com-
merce—Commercial League—English Shipping—Balance of
Trade—Old and New Doctrine of Exports and Imports—Se-
curity of Commerce—Capital—Increase in the Commercial
Prosperity, Production, and Consumption of Great Britain.

London, June 17th, 1835.

WHEN we hear in England, on the one hand, that
trade and manufactures are ruined by injudiciously favouring agriculture, and, on the other,
that agriculture is in the most deplorable condition
from the undue encouragement afforded to commerce and manufactures,—these two conflicting
assertions so contradict or counterbalance each
other, that it is impossible to come to a sound conclusion, without thoroughly examining the several
particulars. The result of this examination is,
that prosperity is the rule for both, and distress
the exception; and that the seat of the evil is
very rarely in the part where it is sought. From
many examples, I select one. There is no subject
on which there have been, in proportion to its importance, such long discussions in Parliament, as
on the glove trade. It was affirmed that, by the
permission to import French gloves, vast numbers
of people had been reduced to ruin and poverty,
&c. What was the result of the inquiry? First,

that many persons now wear silk or cotton gloves, which was an effect of fashion, and had nothing to do with the importation of French leather gloves. Secondly, that not more than a million pairs of such gloves were imported, while more than fifteen million pairs were manufactured in England. Thirdly, that the importation and consumption of skins for gloves had increased of late years. Fourthly, that a duty of twenty-two per cent. was more than sufficient to protect the English glove manufacturer, provided he was not decidedly inferior to the French in skill and taste. But the inferior workmen were the very persons who made the loudest complaints.

The changes in the law did no injury to the cotton-manufacturers, and compelled the silk-weavers and glove-manufacturers to make successful efforts to improve the taste and the quality of their goods. Now, if it appeared impossible and unwise, even with regard to such articles as stockings and gloves, to retain the old system unchanged, how much less can it be done with respect to more important matters and to independent nations? And yet, at a time when the light of day began to break, the Duke of Wellington said, " I shall be the last to propose any change in the system of our commercial relations ; I hope, on the contrary, that this system will be maintained*." He said this at a time when Prussia had already adopted its liberal commercial system, and had induced England to adopt more equitable measures ; though Mr. Robinson af-

* Hansard, xi., 21.

firmed, on the 11th of July, 1831, " Prussia has prohibited all our goods and manufactures *;" whereas the new Tariff prescribes the contrary in express terms.

The times of English monopoly, navigation laws, prohibitions, and all the vexations connected with them, are completely past, and cannot, by any possibility, be restored. The more judicious of the merchants and manufacturers are fully sensible of this. They know that the future grandeur of England is not to be maintained by worn-out ineffective laws, but must rest on other foundations. The loudest opponents are the ship-owners; let us, therefore, hear their arguments, and examine the facts which they allege.

They affirm that the ancient English navigation law, which allowed no nation to import into Great Britain any article except the produce of its own soil and its manufactures,—this law, which is the origin of the immense traffic and naval power of the kingdom, has been madly repealed; and that foreign nations have thus been enabled to outstrip England, and to prepare her ruin. One example will suffice to prove this mathematically :—

EXPENSES.

	In an English Ship.	In a Prussian Ship.
Provisions	£83	£41
The Captain . . .	29	15
The Crew	45	18
All expenses together	345	258

* Hansard, iv. 1034.

That is, 107*l.* greater expense for an English ship. How then shall Great Britain maintain a competition with Prussia? In addition to this, the freight to all parts of the world is so low, compared with former times, that the severest distress of all the ship-owners and navigators is inevitable, or, rather, already exists.

However incontrovertible these statistical data seem to be, they nevertheless prove nothing of what is attempted to be inferred from them. It seems to me that these ship-owners cannot, and will not, rise above the notion, that the *ship,* which is but the *means* of commerce, is to be regarded as the end. This narrow view (which we meet with on the continent in carriers and inn-keepers) was put forward with the utmost confidence and arrogance by one Mr. Powles. He required a monopoly for English ships, and the exclusion, or, at all events, enormous taxation, of all foreign ships. " But," asked Mr. Thompson (the enlightened President of the Parliamentary Committee), " if other nations were to act in the same manner, do you think we should then reap the advantage which you expect ?"—Mr. Powles : " Yes, I do believe it." Mr. Thompson : " Will you tell us how ?"—Mr. Powles : " I beg to be permitted not to answer this question." Pity, that while sailing on in fancied security, this bold seaman should suddenly have run completely aground !

Very different is the language of the ' Edinburgh Review,' a journal which always treats of domestic affairs with sagacity, and discusses foreign affairs with more knowledge and fairness than common. " If we treat independent and powerful nations in such a blind and absurd manner as we have treated Prussia, we must be prepared for the consequences." " It cannot be denied (says another passage) that we have given great provocation to Prussia. Our corn-laws and timber-duties are no less prejudicial to her than they are to ourselves; and, so long as we suffer them to pollute our statute-book, foreign nations will give little credit to our assurances of liberality, and will not be disinclined to check our commerce*."

If Prussia were to apply the principles advocated by the ship-owners, she must prohibit all English goods without exception; instead of that, she has undertaken the struggle for commercial liberty as boldly, and maintained it as steadily, as that for political independence. Prussia, it is true, has not yet completely attained her object; and still less has England yet attained to a completely free trade. But, if we proceed to comparisons, Prussia has much more reason to complain than England. For the Prussian tariff allows the importation of all English goods without exception; and the rates of duty are such, that those goods are met with and sold in all parts of Prussia; whereas in consequence of the English prohibitions or enormous import duties, this is by no means the case with the produce and manufactures of Prussia.

I must here advert to one objection, which might be founded on the Statistical Tables, but yet

* Vol. lviii., p. 281.

K 3

rests upon an erroneous foundation. Those tables show, under the head of Prussia, an extremely small amount of imports from England; hence it is inferred, that the trade with Prussia is very inconsiderable, and that with the rest of Germany, on the contrary, highly important. But the greater part of the goods sent to Germany by way of Rotterdam and Hamburg, find their way into the Prussian dominions, and the heading of those tables proves nothing.

With this error is connected an equally false notion of the Great German Commercial League. Inasmuch as the Prussian states have long since adopted the most liberal system in Europe, no change whatever is effected by that combination; and it is entirely false that it was formed in a spirit of hostility towards England. It might be said with equal justice, that the abolition of duties between England, Scotland, and Ireland, or of those which existed in the interior of France, gave the Germans a right to complain of unfriendly intentions. The more simple and uniform system which Germany, by her own independent will and act, now follows; the abolition of the numerous searches, checks, permits, &c., must eventually be advantageous to England; as, in truth, every rational commercial law has an advantageous influence far beyond the frontiers of the state which adopts it. In the same manner as the Germans will profit by the relieving of the East India trade from oppressive restrictions, the English will profit by the freedom of the German trade. Those only who cannot get above the opinions of ship-owners and carriers will deny this, and will propose measures which, if acted upon systematically, would isolate every nation, and put an end to all commerce.

It is not, however, superfluous to examine more closely into these allegations and facts. Granting, therefore, that these estimates of the expenses of the Prussian and English shipping are correct (and not, for instance, at this moment, with respect to the prices of provisions, incorrect), what follows?   Is a duty of 107*l.* to be imposed upon the Prussian ship?   This would exceed the French licences at the time of Napoleon, and the English orders in council.   And what occasion and inducement would this give to the continent to make counter estimates, on the advantages of machinery, the use of coals, &c.?   We may also be allowed to ask, why are the Prussian sailors to eat, drink, and be clothed worse than the English?   Why is not the important circumstance taken into consideration, that the Prussian ships can earn nothing in the winter, and the English a great deal?   In this mode of proceeding we never come to a clear view of the subject, or at any more satisfactory conclusion, than that the *poorest* nation is, by nature, the *first* commercial nation.   One circumstance alone,—that England possesses larger capitals, and a lower rate of profit, overthrows all these premises and conclusions.

The complaints of the ship-owners, as to the decline of their profits, are answered, in like manner, by simply looking to their outlay :—

	In 1818.			1833.		
---------------------------	£.	s.	d.	£.	s.	d.
1 yard of sail-cloth cost	0	2	3	0	1	9
1 cwt. of iron	0	13	0	1	5,	0
1 cwt.	2	14	0	1	14	0
A barrel of pork . .	6	0	0	0	18	6
1 cwt. of bread . . .	1	5	0	0	18	6

Here, as in so many other cases, we see the great dangers and errors consequent on a one-sided view of things. When, for instance, we look at wages apart from the price of commodities; decrease from increase; receipts from expenditure; profit from capital; capital from profit, and so on, we can never do more than serve the purposes of a party.

Every year new ships are built; besides the articles mentioned above, timber, and many other articles are cheaper: seamen's wages are reduced, and the freight, according to impartial testimony, still produces fair profits. But, indeed, according to the principles of some persons, ships and waggons ought to be burnt, in order to raise the price of freight.

The amount of the lading of ships clearing outwards was, in

	English ships. Tons.	Foreign ships. Tons.
1775 . . .	783,000	64,000
1790 . . .	1,260,000	144,000
1800 . . .	1,269,000	654,000
1815 . . .	1,381,000	751,000
1825 . . .	1,711,000	851,000
1830 . . .	2,102,000	758,000
1831 . . .	2,300,000	896,000

That trade, navigation, and the general intercourse of nations have increased in a manner which
must rejoice every friend of humanity, is beyond
all doubt, and is no more disproved by the fluc-
tuations of particular years, than by the often
erroneous and imperfect statements of statistical
tables.   Some persons have attempted to deduce
from these the fact of the decrease in the number of English ships since the year 1827.   On
more accurate investigation it, however, appeared
that formerly old ships, dismasted and out of condition, had been allowed to stand in the tables.
Ou striking these out, a nearer approach was
made to the truth; the diminished number
proved, not the decay of trade, but the increase of
statistical accuracy.   In the year 1834 the relative
numbers which cleared out were as follows :—

	English.	Tons.	Foreign.	Tons.
London	3421	678,000	1061	175,000
Liverpool	1803	410,000	906	250,000
Bristol	278	51,000	24	5,000
Hull	755	142,600	610	62,600
Newcastle	425	69,000	445	45,000

In the year 1800, 6523 ships sailed from England to Ireland, with 544,000 tons.   In 1834,
14,245 ships, with 1,348,000 tons.

Since 1800, 2213 houses have been built in
Dublin, and most of the towns have increased in
a similar manner.   In a word, in all these particulars England has advanced; and if other nations have roused themselves, have developed
their resources, have produced, bought, and sold,

this is not a ground for envy or complaint, but a source of general congratulation, and general advantage. At any rate, an injudicious perseverance in the old principles of monopoly would not extend, but ruin English commerce.

More enlarged views on these subjects have led to the entire abandonment of the old doctrine of the balance of trade. The prosperity of a nation is no longer inferred, as it used to be, exclusively from the amount of its exports, but much more from its imports. Unless what is brought back is of greater quantity and value than what is taken out, there can be no gain; and so long as there exists any other article of necessity which can be exchanged, money does not appear in the list of exports and imports, or appears only as commodity, as metal, and not as means of mutual adjustment. The doctrine that a nation should buy more than it sells, bring home more than it carries out, may, however, no less than the exploded doctrine, lead to absurd laws (spite of the correction of the error of regarding money as the sole standard of value). We must avoid the egotism of both extremes, and learn at length to see that in every kind of commercial intercourse, both parties must necessarily, in the long run, gain; and that, whenever this is not the case, it inevitably declines. To endeavour to make the gain all on one side is therefore, in fact, to destroy commerce.

The rapid, unexampled, and unexpected profits which many branches of trade made during the war have certainly ceased; but, on the other hand, all branches have gained in security, and commerce is no longer a lottery, but a steady pursuit. If bankruptcies now occur, they are seldom of an inevitable kind, but arise from circumstances independent of the general state of trade; such as insufficient capital, injudicious speculation, expensive modes of living, &c. Every body who can give tolerably good security can easily borrow money at four per cent. ; and it is quite unreasonable to expect to combine the high profits of other times with the low interest of this. People often look only at the subject matter of a trade, and not at the person who carries it on ; and yet, in our days, the results depend as much on the latter as the former.

Mr. Lloyd, the banker, said, " The profits of trade are certainly not large; but when industry, economy, and good judgment are combined, it may still be carried on to advantage." " I do not remember," says Mr. Bates, " ever to have seen the country in so healthy and advantageous a state in regard to trade and manufactures. No crowded warehouses: a brisk demand for every commodity."

Trade and commerce have their unfavourable side, as well as agriculture; and every reasonable man, whether farmer or manufacturer, will lay his account for this; his permanent conclusions cannot and ought not to be drawn from particular moments of prosperity or of adversity. When * the rage for speculation makes men so mad as to send skates and warming-pans to

* Hansard, iv. 924.

Buenos-Ayres, nothing can be done for them; they deserve their ruin.

Follies of this kind are, however, indirect proofs of a redundancy of capital, and from this source, and the greater cheapness of labour (machines included) arises the great superiority of England.

Increase of capital is often the only means of diminishing the cost of production. 20,000*l.* (says a person acquainted with the business) employed in the iron trade will perhaps yield six per cent., whereas 40,000*l.* will give ten. Or, if I make nine per cent. on 100,000 pieces of cloth, I can afford to sell under the market price, and yet have as much profit remaining as formerly, when the cost of production was greater.

I could extract whole sheets of figures, showing the increase and the greatness of the commerce of England, out of the enormous folios of statistical tables which lie before me: but I will let you off with two or three.

In the year 1688, the trade of England amounted to 190,000 tons; in 1790, 1,424,000: in 1820, to 1,668,000; in 1830, to 2,180,000. Even in the year 1829, England possessed 241 steamboats, Scotland 75, and Ireland 26; and these numbers now fall far short of the truth. The value of exported manufactures was, on an average of years,

From	1786-92	.	£14,000,000
	1802-08	.	22,000,000
	1815-19	.	38,000,000
	1830		55,000,000
	1832	.	60,000,000

The exports from Ireland to England were, in the seven years ending 1729, worth 2,307,000*l.* For 1833, to Liverpool alone, 7,456,000*l.*

| Year. | Exports of Great Britain | | Imports. |
	Official Value.	Declared Value.	Declared Value.
1810	32,000,000	46,000,000	30,000,000
1820	32,000,000	34,000,000	29,000,000
1824	43,000,000	36,000,000	34,000,000
1830	55,000,000	35,000,000	42,000,000
1832	60,000,000	36,000,000	48,000,000

This last statement requires explanation. The ' official value' has reference to the prices fixed as unchangeable in the year 1696 : it therefore exhibits only quantities, but it exhibits those with perfect accuracy. Since 1797, however, the merchant has been required to declare the real value, with more or less accuracy, and the rise or fall of the numbers in this list is not an index to quantity, but to price. But as this has fallen, while that has risen, people drew the erroneous inference that commerce generally had declined, and that trade was carried on at a loss. The operation of the price of raw material, the labour performed by machinery, the number of capitals, the rate of interest, &c., vary extremely; but the true, final, important, and satisfactory result is, that now, with diminished means and cost, far greater quantities of commodities are produced, and are sold at far lower prices.

The increase in the consumption of all articles is intimately connected with this fact. I shall perhaps on some future occasion send you more figures, showing this in detail. To-day I conclude with the remark, that if the agriculture of England, viewed in a large and comprehensive manner, and not with reference to transitory evils, is without question in a prosperous state, far more so are the manufactures and commerce.

The condition of the country is artificial, certainly, compared with that more natural state in which men neither sow nor reap, nor weave, nor forge. But the people who are the most skilled in these arts, and carry them on in the largest and most liberal manner, are, at least in these respects, before and above all others. Other nations now move at an accelerated pace in the same track; but their advance is no loss to England, if she will (like Prussia) free herself from the artificial impediments which necessarily arise from corn laws, prohibitions, monopolies, &c.

Much has already been done in this way, and much more will be done; and if the European market for England should contract, a far wider is opened to her since the vast changes in the continent of Asia. Of them another time.

CHAPTER XXXIX.

Malibran in Fidelio—Comparison with Milder, Schechner, Schrœ-
der-Devrient — Variety of Genius — State of the Drama in
England—Causes of its Decline—French, English, and
German Drama—State-Paper Office—Dinners.

London, Tuesday, June 10.

WHEN I read that part of your letter in which
you tell me that our clever and modest friend at
Hähnel said, " I shall now be happy in London
for the first time, for Malibran sings," I felt it as
a weight on my conscience that, in spite of my
extreme admiration, I had not yet heard her.
But hitherto I have been engaged every evening
on which she sang ; and I delayed the more willingly, hoping that I might be able to hear her in
some more genuine work of art than an opera of
Bellini.   And at length Malibran has studied
Fidelio, and last night she appeared in it.

The orchestra is good, although not so full as
at Berlin, nor so attentive to the lights and
shadows; especially to the pianos in accompanying the voice, which it often overpowered.   Let
us proceed to the particular characters.

Mr. Bedford, who acted Don Pizarro, has a
powerful voice, but his performance is wanting in
elevation and refinement.   The passage, " Ein
Stoss und er verstummt," had, from its conception and execution, less effect than with us.   The

chorus of soldiers to the first great aria was very improperly omitted.

Florestan, Mr. Templeton: thin enough, though not quite so starved as he is represented in Germany. The singing such as one could listen to without finding much to praise or to blame.

Jaquino, Mr. Duruset, was somewhat older than usual, and his conception of the part more stolid, impertinent, and ludicrous.

Rocco, Mr. Seguin, is a good singer; but it appears to me that he was mistaken in representing the old gaoler,—who stands in need of an assistant, and who expects to accomplish the murder of Pizarro without violence or difficulty,— as a vigorous, active, and almost facetious man. Our Devrient's acting was masterly in the comparison.

Marcelline, Mrs. Seguin, sung with tolerable correctness, but from time to time rather too loud for the other voices.

The chorus singers, by no means numerous, and the alto again sung by male voices. A fault which I have observed before—that of bawling— recurred here. The loudest singing you ever heard in an opera of Spontini's, and which was justifiable from being in keeping with the rest of the performance, is pianissimo compared to this London screaming and shouting. Perhaps the climate may make it necessary to mix brandy with the pure juice of the grape; but one cannot understand why the beauty and softness of music must be so unmusically concealed by vociferations like those in a booth at a fair. It is, in short, a bad habit, into which even the solo performers fell when singing in the finales.

Lastly—Fidelio, Madame Malibran. It is an inexplicable mystery by what minute details, what indescribable touches, true genius exercises its resistless sway over the minds of men. The moment she came on the stage, this remarkable woman produced the same impression upon me as she had done at Paris. Her appearance was not that of a good-natured peasant lad, a simple rustic gaoler's servant; neither was it that of a woman whose heroic courage and enthusiasm are visible through her mean disguise; she entered, exhausted by the effort of recent labour, and, depositing her burthen, sank upon a seat. While I was pondering whether this conception of the part (which was quite new to me) was the right, she raised her eyes to greet Rocco and Marcelline; and her smile was accompanied with such an indescribable look of the profoundest suffering, the most dignified melancholy, that the tears came into my eyes, before she had uttered a word. This tinge of melancholy, this air of suffering, she retained through the whole part, yet without once falling into a tone of whining sentimentality. In this perfectly original creation and conception of the character—in this sustained and consistent representation of it—she displayed the energy and the influence of genius. There was, of course, no trace of the rusticity of deportment, assumed for the sake of deceiving Rocco, which some actresses have given to the part; none, of the lofty heroical style, or of the womanish coquetry, which have characterized the performance of others.

Her dress was perfectly simple : grey trowsers, a sort of frock coat reaching to the knee, of the same colour, and a black leather girdle. It is almost incomprehensible how so elegantly formed a woman could contrive so entirely to conceal all the feminine graces of her person, that there was nothing to excite even curiosity. She wore no rouge, and her pallid face and dark expressive eyes, with the melancholy tones of her deep and beautiful voice—these, indeed, rivetted eye, and ear, and heart. The moment in which she discovers and resolves what, and how, she has to act, her countenance and demeanour rose into something truly awful.

She spoke English more distinctly and harmoniously than I have ever heard it spoken on the stage. The principal scene of the second (here the third) act was, as usual, the most effective. It would be difficult, if not impossible, to define, in a few words, in what consisted the difference between her performance of it and that of other actresses. Do not conclude from what I say that I am unjust to them; but I can acknowledge no monopoly of genius, and I here saw a fresh proof that it is *creative*. Often and variously as I have seen Fidelio acted, *this* view, *this* representation of the character was entirely new to me—unexpected, and, in itself, perfect.

Milder, with her magnificent tones and person, was more imposing. From the moment she came on the stage you felt and knew that she *must* con-

quer. Schechner's voice was fuller and more profoundly touching. Schrœder-Devrient united the
sweetness and the charm, with the romantic devotion, of woman ; and the torrent of her enthusiasm
bore you along with resistless force.

Malibran betrays the long-suffering, the heart-
wearing anxiety, the dubious mind ; till at length
the strength of her heart and her love overcome
all anxieties and all doubts. To each her own.
Each fulfils the part for which nature, and the character of her genius, has fitted her.

Some ornamented finales found great applause :
they were, doubtless, conceived in a higher style,
and executed with a more perfect feeling of art,
than the other Italian singers here are capable of ;
but yet they had no business there. The words,
" *Was in mir vorgeht ist unaussprechlich*," by
which Schrœder-Devrient always produces so astonishing an effect, Malibran gave in an unimpres-
sive, almost a conversational, tone ; but in the
passage in which she and Florestan sink on their
knees, she expressed pious gratitude, united with
conjugal tenderness, in the most beautiful manner.
So long as Pizarro remains in the prison, her eye
never quits him, and she keeps the pistol pointed
at him till he goes out.

I could tell you of many other little touches
and peculiarities, but what I have said will suffice
to give you an idea of the total impression. There
is, indeed, no greater enjoyment than that
of seeing and understanding the *variety* of genius. All exclusive inspiration, which arrogates
to itself supremacy, is, in fact, but of a sub-

ordinate class.   Why should I forget the Niebe-
lungen because I admire Homer? decry Shakspeare in behalf of Sophocles, or Handel in that of
Mozart? Why close my ears to the perfections of
one singer, because there exists in the world another of merit?   I have often found that a singer
imagined I was become cold or hostile to her, or
thought I had lost my taste and judgment, because I commended another!   This is a great
error.   He who is incapable of analysing and
appreciating various peculiarities and different
merits, cannot comprehend the true character of
any individual one, but contents himself with a
shallow and selfish traffic of flattery.   Never was
I more profoundly sensible of the grandeur of
Sophocles than when fresh from Shakspeare;
never did I more love and admire Shakspeare
than when the music of the trimeters and choruses of Sophocles was still upon my ear!   And
so I was never more sensible to the merits of the
singers I allude to, never more grateful for the
delight they have given me, than last night, when
Malibran said or sang to me ' Anch' io son pittore.'

Fidelio was succeeded by what pretended to be
a farce, ' Turning the Tables.'   It was, however,
so tediously spun out, and so poorly performed,
that I went away before the end.

You find two opinions on almost everything in
England; on one point alone all seem agreed—
that the stage has declined, and is declining.
It has attracted the attention even of parliament.
A committee heard the evidence of many persons
the most interested and the best informed on the

subject, drew up a report, and made some pro-
positions; but parliament took no decisive step,
and all goes on in the same bad course. It is
doubtful, indeed, whether any act of legislation
can effectually renovate art, or save it from irremediable decay. In the reports in question, and
in some periodical works, the most different reasons are alleged for the decline of the drama;
and I have a few more, which I must beg to add
to the number.

1. Many pieces which are represented are in-
decorous and immoral, and even lovers of dramatic amusement are thus kept away, or at any
rate deterred from taking their wives and daughters. This, it is true, is less a cause of the evil,
than an evil of which the causes remain to be
sought out. Some are of opinion that the good
sense and sound taste of the public will reject
this noxious stuff; and this may be true of the
sound and moral portion of it; but experience
shows that the friends of everything coarse, the
populace, sometimes gain complete supremacy in
the theatre; that whole generations revel in this
dissoluteness (as in the time of Charles II.), or that
poets and those who give the tone to public opinion (as we now see in France) pander to the lowest
and grossest tastes and passions. Hence others
maintain that nothing can prevent this evil, and
avert the danger of universal corruption, but a
preventive censorship, or dramatic police. If
this were employed in a temperate and rational
manner, and not perverted by party feelings and
purposes, it could hardly excite a murmur; and,

indeed, such a power has been beneficially exercised in some instances by the Lord Chamberlain, or his deputy. The latter, however, it must be said, made himself ludicrous, by striking out the words " she is an angel," on the ground of its being impious and shocking to apply this sacred epithet to a woman.

2. The theatres, and the neighbourhood of them, are crowded with a revolting multitude of loose women. This nuisance might easily be abated ; at all events, it must be a very subordinate cause of the degeneracy of the dramatic art.

3. A great number of persons hold it sinful, on religious grounds, to go to the theatre. These persons misinterpret Christianity, and misunderstand art, when they confound its highest manifestations with its perversions, and regard both with the same eye. They are, however, perfectly right in pronouncing the most complete condemnation against that foul sort of dramatic literature, which declares war upon the good, the true, and the beautiful.

4. The encouragement given to the theatre by former sovereigns, particularly by George III., who frequently visited it, had a very beneficial effect. The want of this example has caused the theatre to be deserted by the fashionable world, and this has been equally injurious to the taste and to the exchequer of the theatre. No king can create art by a miracle,—but he may give it most important encouragement and support. The kings of Prussia and Bavaria have found to their own satisfaction, and to the delight of others, how much

may be done by this honourable patronage of art.

5. The great increase of novels, and other sorts of light reading, diminishes the interest in the theatre.

The mass of literary instruction and amusement is undoubtedly much greater than ever it was; but I do not think that this would destroy the attraction of the theatre, were not the former very cheap, and the latter very dear.

6. The costliness of theatrical amusements is a material ground of the comparatively small number of those who resort to them; and this costliness again grows out of an ill-judged encouragement of taste for *spectacle*, to the detriment of all higher poetical objects : dress, decorations, processions, fireworks, and other mere shows, are employed to conceal the miserable deficiency of the main requisites.

7. Concerts and the opera draw away a great many who would visit the theatre. These morning concerts are certainly in entire defiance of the principle, that amusement is to come after the duties and labours of the day have been fulfilled; and generally consist of a superficial, incongruous *pasticcio*, which has little to do with real art, and, at the very best, can only borrow the slightest merit or meaning from the brilliancy or the glitter of certain "stars." The opera, however, whatever be its apparent prosperity or splendour, is itself in a state of degeneracy and poverty of art. London spends but too much money to hear two or three *undramatic* operas out of the manu-

factory of the day. But what has this to do with music and its exhaustless treasures, which, under skilful and judicious management, might be brought to light, and made the property of the public ?

8. Dramatic writers are comparatively ill paid, and have no protection for their literary property. Men of genius and talent, therefore, betake themselves to other branches of literature. The pay of dramatic authors is very various and uncertain; and all the provincial theatres may take possession of a piece which has been acted in London, without paying the author anything.

9. The theatres are grown to so unnatural a size, that it is impossible to see or hear distinctly. On their examination, Kean and Kemble declared themselves in favour of large houses : they said that the actor moved with more freedom; that the higher order of tragedies required great space, and the nearness of the actors to the audience destroyed the illusion.

When Kean maintained that distance concealed the defects of an actor, he forgot that it equally obscured his excellencies, destroyed all the more delicate inflexions of the voice and the countenance, and rendered vain the finer expressions of gesture.

A remark, or an inference of Kemble's is equally inconclusive. He says, when the Haymarket Theatre is quite full, and Drury-Lane is (as often happens) three-quarters full, those who sit on the back benches are equally remote from the actors. In this case, the cost of building for the other fourth might and ought to have been spared. And it is by no means the same thing, whether an actor speaks in a space, less by a fourth. It cannot be doubted that the size of the houses first led to the introduction of mere shows; seeing became the first object, and the dramatic art the second. They have also immensely increased the expenses, both incidental and regular; have raised the price of admittance, and materially contributed to the bankrupt condition of their proprietors.

10. The hours of dining interfere with those of the theatre. This circumstance is one of great importance, for it operates almost to the exclusion of the more refined classes, and throws the ascendancy, and the power of deciding on the merits of the performance into the hands of the uncultivated. If the play were to begin earlier, it would interfere with the hours of business; if later, there is an end to all night whatever; and a man who does not sleep by night cannot work by day. It seems a question, whether it would not be better to reduce the performance from five or six hours to three (as with us), and to lower the prices, than to admit the lower classes at so late an hour for half-price. Parliament, and the numerous societies and meetings which assemble in an evening, also keep a great proportion of the educated classes from the play.

11. It is a bad thing that there are no police regulations as to the number of tickets issued. There are often more tickets sold than there is room to admit; and a man who has been forced

to stand in a crowd, and to see nothing, is not
eager to go again. The long waiting and squeez-
ing at the doors is also extremely unpleasant,·
and must be more so to the busy English than
to other people, who have more time and more·
patience.

12. Political excitement makes men indifferent
to the theatre.

There is doubtless a high and noble, as well as
a diseased political excitement; and the former
throws not only the drama, but everything, else
in the world, into the background.   But we find
this united with the greatest dramatic enthusiasm
among the Greeks; while other nations made no
greater progress in dramatic literature, because
they were deficient in political spirit. This, indeed, is nearly connected with the question, how
far the stage is susceptible of a political tendency
and colour, or how far it ought to receive it.
This is a question of degree. It is too much, when
art forgets her own dignity and independence,
and makes herself a mere instrument; too little,
when one of the most momentous elements of
dramatic elevation and effect is entirely excluded.
Comedy, at all events, must treat of the present,
and must be privileged to make it her own. The
time is past when any effect could be produced
by defrauded wards, bribed chambermaids, and
the like.   But it is not only the characters,
foibles, and absurdities of kings of the present
age, that are withdrawn from the pen of the dramatist; every new-made minister, every canting
priest, every conceited professor, every world-

reforming innovator, every drivelling adorer of antiquity, declares himself sacrosanct, and maintains that no poet has a right profanely to peer into his holy circle. Nay, the very players themselves, whose business it is to parody every variety of mankind, call out if their weaknesses are made ridiculous.

13. The monopoly of Drury-Lane and Covent-Garden has injured or crushed the other theatres. Where there is no competition, no emulation, there will be no artists, and the taste of the public for the theatre will consequently decline.

Whether, and in what degree, these theatres possess an exclusive right, is a matter that has been much contested. There is no doubt that they themselves have believed in the existence of this right, and that others, in the same belief, have lent them large sums of money, for which there is now no adequate security, but which would utterly vanish if the monopoly were destroyed, without any compensation. Several theatres have been licensed only on condition that they are not to perform the *legitimate* drama. But nobody can say what is this forbidden legitimate drama, or what the permitted burletta. Shakspeare's ‘Othello,’ for instance, was transformed into a burletta, by having a man seated at a pianoforte behind the scenes, who, about every quarter of an hour, at the shifting of the scenes, struck a few chords as softly as possible. Is it not absurd, say the defenders of the freedom of the drama, to enjoin that the perfect, the classical drama, should be performed only in one

place, while all others are condemned to the imperfect, the unartistical? Why may every bad
translation of a bad French play or vaudeville
be represented everywhere, and Shakspeare and
Massinger only in an enormous house, where
people will not go to hear them, because they
cannot hear them if they do go? It were surely
far better to relegate all the bad and objection-
able to one theatre, and to throw open every stage
to the excellent. This foolish monopoly has
no other effect than to make people pay the
highest price for the worst things: whereas free
competition would produce the best representations at the lowest prices; exclusive rights, of this
kind, never increased incomes, nor created capital; they produce nothing but conceit and negli-
gence. " I possess," said Mr. Warburton, " a
500*l.* share, for which I never received one penny
interest. On the contrary, I have to advance
money to maintain a useless establishment, in-
debted three times its value, or look for repay-
ment from the sale of the old dresses and the
benches. I should willingly give up my capital,
if I could but see more rational laws for the
theatre, and the removal of all restrictions on the
drama." "Free competition," remarked another
person, " will prove where the greatest talents,
the most refined taste, and the greatest industry
are to be found."

These and similar arguments were met by the
assertion that the decline both in acting and in
prosperity, of Drury Lane and Covent Garden,
was attributable, not only to the licence granted

to small theatres to act, but to the opening of
many without a licence. The attempts of the great
theatres to assert their rights in a legal way
failed, because the expenses were so enormous,
that the decision usually found them bankrupt.
The public, too, generally took part with the
defendants. The multiplication of theatres does
not increase the number of artists, nor of ama-
teurs, and low prices only deteriorate the quality
of the audience, and submit every thing to the
judgment of the uneducated.

Wearied with the length of these discussions,
some enemies of all theatrical amusements came
forward, and observed, that the law, even so late
as in George the Second's time, placed " players,
vagabonds, and rogues" on the same footing. Mr.
Rotch said " the theatres answered no other purpose than that of collecting together players—a
wretched set of outcasts, who have no other
means of subsistence;—and we are to take the
trouble to legislate for such sort of people ! "

" What," another asked, " is the best way of
filling the houses ?" " Dress a girl, who has handsome legs, in men's clothes; she will bring £80
at the half-price," was his reply.

Highly as first-rate talent is paid here, second-
rate is paid extremely ill. The utmost given in
provincial theatres is three guineas a week. The
salaries are, generally, much less than this, and
the actors have to buy their own dresses.

A table of the receipts of Covent Garden shows
a great variation of prices, the highest of which
is, in the year 1811, £98,000, while in the year

1831-2, it has not exceeded £43,000. The table shows on the whole a great falling off; but the sudden rise in some years, and fall in others, shows the effect of good or bad management, or of the talents of a great actor. Whence, otherwise, a falling off of £19,000 between the years 1819 and 1820, and the following year again a rise of £15,000? or a difference of £16,000 between the years 1829 and 1830? There is, however, no corresponding table of expenditure; and without this it is impossible to know whether the years of increased receipt were also years of greater profit.

The Report of the parliamentary committee on the state of the Drama contains a statement of the size of various theatres, from which I extract the following :—

	From the curtain to the centre box. Feet.	Greatest breadth of the pit. Feet.
Drury Lane	61	50
Covent Garden	63	50
Haymarket	47	35
Italian Opera	90	62
Dublin	52	45
Tottenham Street	38	22
St. Carlo, Naples	79	63
Scala, Milan	90	67
Cirque Olympique	86	83
Théâtre des Variétés	52	43
Odéon	71	60
Feydeau	64	52
Théâtre Français	61	55

A very mistaken opinion has been put forth

that, though playhouses may be too large, opera-
houses cannot.   You may, to be sure, increase
the strength of the orchestra, but not the voices
of the singers; and hence the hard and toneless
shouting and screaming, and the rapid destruction of voice.

On a retrospect of all the causes which have
been assigned for the decline of dramatic art,
they seem to me more than sufficient to account
for its present deplorable state.   I even fear that
the grand remedy proposed—the young lady in
men's clothes—will also soon lose its efficacy.
Whether, however, the causes assigned be really
the primary ones, and not themselves consequences of causes which lie deeper, is still open
to inquiry.   When, for instance, it is said that
people do not go to the play, *because* they dine at
that hour, it might, with equal truth, be said of
another period, people do *not* dine at such or
such an hour, *because* they go to the play: therefore, 'as these two *becauses* neutralize each other,
we must find a third and a more satisfactory one.

If some nations have no dramatic poetry, and
if others, after possessing, lose it, these are indications of very different causes and peculiarities.
Notwithstanding the many similarities in the circumstances of the theatres in England, France,
and Germany, the tastes and opinions of the
three countries are, in some respects, entirely
at variance.   The exclusive direction of the national activity to the practical and material side
of life cannot be favourable to poetry in England;
—least of all to dramatic poetry, which absolutely

requires a certain time to be allotted to it.. The
pungent political herbs which the French strew
over their stage are not plants of a poetical soil;
still less can the delicate flower of beauty and of
poetry grow—as they would have us believe—out
of the rank and pestilent mass of corruption
which they have heaped together.

. On the German soil everything takes root;
and, for that very reason, nothing is indigenous;
yet the utter anarchy of our theatre seems to me
better than the despotism of France, or the indifference of England. But a vast deal more might
be effected by intelligent managers, really masters of their business, and themselves not devoid
of originality and poetry; by rigorous rejection
of middling or bad actors; by encouragement
of really good ones; by judicious cast of parts;
by rejection of inferior pieces, &c., than is generally imagined. I cannot see the advantage to
the Berlin royal theatre in the monopoly it is
permitted to exercise against that of Königstadt,
also a king's theatre. Their own sound judgment and free choice ought to lead each of
them to adopt a different sphere, beyond which
it would be injurious to themselves to .venture;
but this has a very different effect from the
compulsory restraints which paralyse their exertions. Unfettered emulation is favourable to
art, and stimulates the public interest; so that
in the end, all parties gain, and none lose.

It is the province of the stage, says Aristotle,
to chastise and purify the passions. Instead,
however, of holding in veneration this purifica-

tion by the bright and refining fire of art, too
many seek in the theatre only a confirmation of
their own groveling and vulgar passions; these
react again upon the drama, till the lowest,
coarsest, and most atrocious of the spectators
may esteem himself pure and holy compared to
the heroes of the pseudo poets. What an anti-
climax! The genuine stage exhibits nature more
noble, more sublime than in her wonted course;
then comes a time when the audience will look
at nothing but the image and reflexion of themselves; and lastly, they require the exhibition of
crimes and vices of every kind, in order that they
may exult in the contrast of their own excellence!

There is no art which demands such a power
of self-oblivion and self-abnegation in him who
would understand it, as the dramatic art. Such
a talent of throwing the whole of the thoughts
and feelings into other natures and other circumstances! In this respect the qualities required in
an historian and a dramatist are similar; though
the mode of treating and of presenting the sub-
ject-matter appears, in other respects, completely
opposed. All abstraction, whether historical, political, philosophical, or religious, is undramatic.

*   *   *   *   *

London, June 18.

I was interrupted, fortunately perhaps; for my
epic discourse on the drama must already have
tired you.

To return to my daily history.—My labours in
the State Paper Office go on prosperously; and

perhaps it is conducive to my health that the time
of work is circumscribed to between the hours of
eleven and three. I have chosen the period of
1740—1763 to begin with, as it forms a continuation to my extracts from the Mitchell papers.
The dispatches from the principal kingdoms of
Europe throw light on each other; and I hope
that, when I have arranged every thing, I shall
be able to delight you as well as myself with my
spoil.

I went to dine with Mr. T—— the day before yesterday; he had given me permission to
come uninvited when I had no other engage-
ment. This friendly unceremonious reception is
very agreeable and convenient.

Yesterday I was invited, first, to the dinner of
a society at Freemasons' tavern, and, secondly,
to Mr. M——; whilst I was pondering upon the
course I should take in this *embarras de richesses*,
a third invitation from the Duke of S—— decided
the affair. About this and my further fortunes I
will write next time. For to-day, adieu.

LETTER XL.

Milbank Penitentiary—Extravagant Diet of Prisoners—Compulsory Silence—Crime and Punishment—Increase of Crime in.
England — Value of Statistical Details — Increase of Minor
Offences, Decrease of Atrocious Crimes—Effect of Mitigation.
of Punishments — Reform of Criminal Law — Sir J. Mackintosh—Sir Robert Peel—English Mode of Codification—Punishment of Death—Comparative Statements of Committals and
Convictions — Forgery — Imprisonment for Debt — Scotland—
Ireland.

London, June 9, 1835.

I HAVE had an opportunity of seeing the General
Penitentiary, which is situated at the western extremity of London.   It consists of one building
in the centre of a very spacious court, and six
other hexagonal buildings connected with it.
This form was selected from its affording, according to Bentham's opinion, the greatest facilities for inspection.   Whether it be the best, is
a question I cannot go into.   The fundamental
idea of the whole institution is, that a number of
criminals may, by judicious treatment, be reformed
and brought back to virtue.   The government,
under whose immediate direction it is, decides
what persons are to be admitted, and reserves to
itself the right of rewarding the good behaviour
of the prisoners by shortening the term of their
imprisonment.

The Penitentiary is directed by a board appointed by the king. Under this board, with

different powers and duties, are, a governor, or inspector, sub-inspector, chaplain, schoolmaster, physician, masters for the work, keepers, turn-keys, &c. The rule of silence is enforced here, as far as it is possible. The occupations, chiefly sewing and tailor's work, are carried on in the separate cells. Some few only, such as grinding corn, washing, baking, &c. by several together. The treadmill, used merely as a punishment, and not with any view to production, has very properly been rejected. The profits of the labour are given three-fourths to the establishment, one-eighth to the prisoners, and one-eighth to the superintendent of the work. The prisoners are divided into two classes, distinguished by their dresses: those in the first, and those in the last half of their term of imprisonment. A very exact register is kept of their conduct, and the result accelerates or retards their liberation. No one, however, is dismissed in less than three years. The occupations for the whole day are accurately laid down. Each prisoner eats alone in his cell. For breakfast he has milk porridge, and half-a-pound of bread. For dinner, one day, two ounces of cheese and a pound of bread, with onions; three days, a quart of meat broth with oatmeal, rice, peas, &c. and potatoes, and half-a-pound of bread; three days, the same quantity of potatoes and bread, and six ounces of meat, with half-a-pint of broth. The supper is the same as the breakfast. All the officers of the establishment must belong to the Church of England.

On these brief details I must remark—

First,—If we calculate the value of the ground, the enormous building, the number of persons employed, and the cost of feeding the prisoners, the result will be such an extravagant expenditure, that every rogue there costs more than a travelling chorister or young artist *. It would be difficult to find in the whole world so expensive an educational establishment.

Secondly,—Philanthropists have made very laudable efforts to mitigate the hardness and cruelty which formerly reigned within the walls of a prison. But I must repeat here the censures which were called forth by the consideration of the poor-laws, on the preposterous mistake of giving the criminal better food and less work than the independent labourer. And not only do these thieves, or whatever they may be, eat, drink, sleep, and lodge better than most of the independent peasantry of the continent, but better even than very many of the independent labourers of England; and certainly than the whole unfortunate population of Ireland. There are scarcely a hundred of the most opulent families in Berlin, who consume such fine wheaten bread as the prisoners here think they have a right to demand. This proceeding can hardly be justified on any principles of penal jurisprudence, or of political economy; not even indeed, by the scriptural example of the prodigal son. The fatted calf was killed when he was a

---

* Small salaries or allowances are granted by most or all of the German governments to young men without fortune, who travel with a view to improvement in the particular art to which they devote themselves.—*Translator.*

true and reformed penitent, but not every day while he was yet a sinner.

Thirdly,—What is done in the way of reformation, particularly by the influences or exercises of religion, is not more than is, or ought to be, done in every prison or house of correction whatever. Silence and compulsory labour, in themselves, afford no means and no proof of reformation. A man who has on one occasion broken this silence, and been in consequence longer imprisoned, may stand higher in the scale of morality, than one whose silence may be the mere effect of stupidity or obstinacy, though it may obtain him approbation and liberty.

Fourthly,—A great number of the prisoners are boys and girls, who have committed one act of theft, generally under momentary excitement and temptation. I cannot but think it an unfortunate and unjust penal system which condemns such criminals to years of imprisonment; and a most inefficient means of reformation to shut them up in a solitary cell, to work in gloomy silence. Would it really be a greater barbarity to do like our forefathers,—give these boys a good sound whipping, and trust their reformation to external causes, than thus to rob them of the faculty of speech, and transform them into dumb animals by way of making them men?

In all these arrangements there appears to me a great mistake of the judicious with the absurd.

The transition from this subject to the more general one of crimes and punishments is natural, and I am the more strongly tempted to enter upon it, from the notion which commonly prevails on the continent of the demoralization of England, and the ruin by which she is threatened from the great increase of crime. As many political quacks prescribe the same remedy, and in the same proportions, for the most different diseases, (such, for instance, as what they call a constitution, and that for all states,) so there are quacks of the contrary kind, who have a dozen different mortal causes for the *one death* which can come but once. According to their predictions, England is dying of poor-laws, of Catholic emancipation, of the reform-bill, of municipal reform, of taxes, debt, drunkenness, above all, of crime. I have given you what information I could collect on some of these subjects, and I shall endeavour, by degrees, to send you something on all. We will keep now to the latter. Drunkenness I have spoken of already; and I have only to add that, in the middle and higher classes, this vice has greatly declined; and that though the Germans were, for centuries, notoriously more addicted to it than the Spaniards or the Italians, they did not, therefore, fall into rapid decrepitude and extinction. I have not the smallest doubt that good regulations with regard to the sale of beer, and a different way of keeping the sabbath, would very greatly diminish this evil.

But the crimes, I hear the objectors say—the crimes! Do you mean, in your excessive partiality for England, to deny them altogether? or, perhaps, to transform them into virtues? In the year 1805, there were 4605 committals, and 2783 convictions; in 1831, 19,647 committals, and 13,830 convictions. These few lines of arithmetic confute all your sophistries, and lay open to view an abyss whose existence the blind alone can deny;—whose terrific aspect none but the moral indifferentist, or the revolutionary leveller, who thinks such a state of corruption and decomposition the necessary prelude to political regeneration, can fail to recognize.

Spite of this anathema, I venture into the lists against the arithmetic, and all the consequences deduced from it. It is doing excellent service to introduce certainty into what is uncertain, and to clear up and confirm obscure and vacillating opinions by means of figures. But do these abstract numbers always preserve a sufficiently characteristic value? Are there no such things as arithmetical mistakes? And are not these more likely to occur in political science, than in the astronomical speculations of Ptolemy or Tycho Brahe? Or, may I not draw wrong conclusions from right data? or entirely lose sight of facts which co-operate in an important degree towards the production of a result attributed exclusively to one? Before people pin their faith with such superstitious reverence on figures, they should most carefully examine how they are obtained, and what is their exact value. The following thesis may serve as matter for a discussion, the result of which will, I hope, be, to bring us nearer to the truth.

First,—All the older tables on the statistics of England are notoriously imperfect and inaccurate; so that a comparison of former and more recent figures lead to no safe inference. According to them, for example, before the year 1828, no case of stealing by day, accompanied with forcible entrance into a house, had ever occurred in England. In general it may be observed that, in the statistics of early times (as in accounts of censuses, poll-taxes, &c.), the numbers are too small, because there were considerable omissions, and no one was counted twice.

Secondly,—No inference can be drawn with safety, nor any average taken, as to the general moral condition of the country, from the tables which have been carefully drawn up for the last few years. Or, what conclusion do we arrive at? That, in the year 1820 alone, 272 persons were prosecuted for having in their possession forged bank notes; and that in the years from 1830 to 1833—that is, in four years—only two persons. Or, on the other hand, that for ten consecutive years there was not a single instance of breaking machinery, while, in the year 1831, 665 persons were prosecuted for this offence; in the year 1833, again, only one individual.

Thirdly,—The magnitude and importance of crime varies so extremely, that a mere addition sum, whether for former or latter times, gives no satisfactory information. A much more material question is, what are the kinds of crime that have increased? what that have decreased? And here we find (independently of all other causes) the great increase to consist in the number of the lesser offences against property, while atrocious crimes have diminished. For example, the number of persons prosecuted for

Simple theft were, in 1820	6499	1833	9818
Housebreaking by night }	283	..	68
Murder . ..	11	..	7
High Treason .	33		0
Child-stealing . „	3	„	0

From these examples I do not presume to deduce universal conclusions, but one which is undeniable in this case,—that totals of different crimes decide nothing whatever as to the greater or less demoralization of a country; but that one must value, weigh, and ponder, whether one case of murder or high treason does not lie as heavy in the balance as a hundred petty thefts.

Fourthly,—Alterations in certain laws (*e. g.* game and excise laws) occasion the rise or fall of whole classes of crimes and punishments. This is a circumstance to which too little attention has been paid.

Fifthly,—The number of prosecutions has increased considerably, from the circumstance that the injured party is no longer, as formerly, exposed to the danger of paying costs far exceeding the amount of the injury. If, for instance, a man was robbed of the value of a pound, he submitted, because it would have cost him at least six to prosecute.

Sixthly, — An increased number of prosecutions also arises from the mitigation of punishments, and especially the abolition of the punishment of death for simple theft. Formerly a person who was robbed scrupled to expose a fellow-creature to the risk of being hanged for a few shillings; and juries had equal reluctance to pronounce a verdict of guilty. The removal of these two latter causes has greatly increased the number of criminals *brought to justice;* but this proves nothing at all as to the number of crimes *committed.*

Seventhly,—Till within a few years no police, properly so called, has existed in England. Since the introduction of it, a multitude of offences are discovered and punished, which formerly went unpunished.

Eighthly,—The population has greatly increased within the last few years; and this has of course affected the number of crimes. Upon these various grounds, judges and magistrates of various degrees, and governors of the great prisons maintain, that, (regard being had to quality as well as number of crimes,) if it is too much to assert that the morality of England has improved, at least the proofs of increasing vice and crime deduced from the figures above quoted are superficial and inconclusive.

And now, since, if we have not actually arrived at truth, we have made some approach to it, and have rectified our point of view, all sorts of detached observations present themselves. This is no place for an accurate or full statement of English criminal law or criminal procedure. There is no doubt that they greatly needed reforms, and that they need them still. The punishment of death, for example, was attached to 160 different offences, till, in the year 1819, a Committee of the House of Commons, of which Sir James Mackintosh was chairman, first laboured at the amelioration and mitigation of these laws. Sir Robert Peel rendered a similar service to the country in 1826, when, by his law regarding theft, a hundred and forty other laws were abrogated.

This is the way in which codification is carried on in England—bit by bit.—One important point is taken up after another, and treated separately; and it never occurs to anybody to see any evil in this course.

That the new laws were strictly in harmony with the spirit and events of the age is clearly proved from this : that what is now regularly expressed by law was formerly irregularly effected by Royal pardon. In the thirty years succeeding the year 1688, the number of those condemned to death, compared to those executed, was as . . . . 38 to 20

From 1755 to 1784 . . 46 „ 13
„ 1784 „ 1814 . . 74 „ 19

The punishment of death is now adjudged by law for burglary above the value of 5*l.*; stealing from shipwrecked vessels; horse, cattle, and sheep stealing; robbery, murder, treason, arson, coining, and a few other offences.

In the seven years ending
with 1819, were executed 662
1826 „ 528
1833 391

The numbers executed in London are,

1827	.	33	1831	. 6
1828	.	17	1832	. 4
1829	.	21	1833	. 6
1830	.	25	1834	. 2

Criminals of every class, tried and condemned in London and Middlesex:

1827	.	2300	1831	. 2372
1828	.	2277	1832	. 2653
1829	.	2318	1834	. 2686
1830	.	3227		

In the year 1820, 1655 persons were transported for seven years; in the year 1833, 2546.

In the year 1820, 107 were executed; in the year 1833, only 32.

In the year 1820, 4089 persons were condemned to six months imprisonment; in the year 1833, 7618. This is, therefore, the period of the greatest increase of prosecutions and convictions.

In the year 1833, 23,787 persons were arrested for intoxication; in 1832, 25,702; in 1833, 18,487; 7754 of whom were women. This increase, perhaps, arose partly from the abolition of a former tax on beer—the diminution, from the balance being restored, and from the establishment of a stricter police.

In the year 1832, 77,543 persons were arrested for various offences; in the year 1833, 69,959; the diminution, therefore, is 7584.

No education, and, least of all, the mere knowledge of reading and writing, can extirpate crime; yet the number of criminals is much greater

among the ignorant. For an example, out of
197 prisoners, only 64 could read; out of 400,
250 might be called totally uneducated*. The
proportion that female criminals bore to male
ones was, in the years 1812-19, as 13 to 58; in
1819-26, as 15 to 80; in 1826-33, as 21 to 110.
According to a report, there was one criminal
each year, in

England	on	740	persons.
Wales	„	2320	„
Scotland	„	1130	„
Ireland	„	490	„
Cardiganshire . . .	„	4930	„
Northumberland . .	„	2700	„
London and Middlesex	„	400	„
Dublin	„	96	„

Setting aside all doubt as to the accuracy of
these figures, I must again remark that, here again,
crimes of the most different magnitude are collected together into one sum-total; and that
these numbers, consequently, afford no test of
general guilt and innocence. It is impossible
that as many petty thefts can occur in Cardigan-
shire as in London, for the simple reason, that
the objects of theft do not exist. But those who,
for the sake of diminishing the number of certain
offences, would loosen the stricter bonds of social
life, scatter men over the face of the country, or
preserve their innocence by keeping them on a
desert island,—these apparent philanthropists forget that a view of the world, with relation only

* Hansard, xiii. 621; xvi. 637.

to criminal law, is a very narrow and partial one; that the advantages of a higher civilization and nearer social intercourse increase in a greater ratio than the disadvantages; or that, if the shadows are sharper, it is precisely because the lights are brighter. Uncivilized people commit more crimes than civilized ones; and even were this not the case, their whole existence (inasmuch as it does not fulfil the vocation of man) is pitiable and abortive. Degenerate, enervated nations are doubtless far below savages, because they want the vigour necessary to regeneration, and because the consciousness of decline aggravates all the evils of it; but the entire removal of temptations to crime could only be effected by the destruction of many of the most valuable possessions and privileges of social life.

Among the celebrated lawgivers of antiquity, Draco tried to renovate and invigorate the whole state by means of criminal law. Events, however, proved that Solon's system, which was rather to promote and preserve the health of the many, than to eradicate the local diseases of the few, was far more successful. Not less inapplicable is the abstract doctrine of the Stoics, who considered every departure from the right as equally wrong; inasmuch as the right was one, and therefore it was indifferent how far removed from right anything might be, so that it *was* removed. According to this doctrine, every arithmetical error is equally wrong; and yet a merchant, who miscalculates to the amount of a penny, is not ruined, because he would be bankrupt if he was in error to the amount of 100,000*l.*

The same may be affirmed of morals; and it is a great advance in English criminal law, that it no longer adjudges the same extreme punish- ment to crimes of the most different magnitude.

The question, whether the punishment of death should be retained in cases of forgery, gave occa- sion to very remarkable proceedings. A thou- sand bankers petitioned for its abolition, on the ground that it did *not* protect their property. They affirmed that it was almost impossible to find witnesses willing to give evidence, or juries to convict. Of ten accused, about one was convicted and punished; while, in cases of prosecution for murder, nine out of ten were convicted, and only one acquitted. So also, eleven hundred jurymen declared that they esteemed it a greater wrong to sentence a man to death for forgery, than to equi- vocate with their oath in such cases. In conse- quence of these and other expressions of public opinion, the punishment of death for forgery was abolished in August, 1832; and only two sorts of forgery remain capital,—forgery of wills, and for- gery of powers of attorney for the transfer of stock*.

That part of English law which regards im- prisonment for debt has been considered pecu- liarly open to reprobation. In two years and a half, ten thousand persons were imprisoned in London, at an expense of from 150,000*l.* to

---

* Hansard, xiv. 969. 1393.

200,000*l.*, and most of them for this cause :—
credit is given in the most incautious manner—
often dishonestly offered; and then the tyranny
of private property (the only thing considered in
the matter) is asserted with such rigour, that
vast numbers are torn from their occupations,
deprived of all means of subsistence, and totally
ruined. Even Lord Eldon (who is not accused
of being a rash innovator) said, " the law of
imprisonment for debt is a license to act in a
manner more injurious and inhuman than was
ever done towards slaves*."

Here again I come to a matter in which legislation, by its very apparent abstract equality, becomes infinitely more oppressive to the poor than
to the rich. This naturally produces feelings of
hostility to the law; and this, again, tends to
produce revolutionary convulsions, which greater
care to maintain equal justice would altogether
avert.

In Scotland, as well as in England, theft is by
far the most common offence. It is, however,
characteristic that, among 1808 persons who were
prosecuted in the course of a year, 484 were committed for assault. About half were found guilty,
and sentenced; generally, to three months' imprisonment.

Causes of the most different description doubtless contribute to increase the number of crimes
in Ireland. In the year 1822, we find 7512 persons convicted; and this number had risen, in

---

* M‘Culloch's Dictionary, Art. ' Credit.'

1832, to 9759.. 'Assault' here plays a much more conspicuous part. Under this head we find, in 1822, 2313; and, in 1832, 3193 prosecutions. Spite of the deplorable confusion and agitation of recent times, the number of cases of murder has fallen from 74 to 31, whilst that of misdemeanours has risen from 1106 to 1734. In 1822, 101 persons were executed; in 1832, only 39. In the sum-total of Irish criminals, many years exhibit full a thousand illicit distillers of whisky.

The blame of all these things, and of others which are notorious, falls partly on the government, partly on the people. As soon as the former grants an equal measure of justice *to all*, the latter will become better and more peaceable; or, if that expectation should fail, they may be constrained to observe law and order in a very different manner from what has hitherto been possible.

London, June 21.

As my other reports were long enough, this has lain by me, and I now add a remark or two on the blank page.

It is not true that the rise or fall of the morality of a people can be measured by certain phenomena, which, if I may use the expression, stand at the very outermost limits of civil society. Such an extreme fact is crime. The morality or immorality of by far the greater number of men lies within the verge of crime, and may undergo many changes and much depreciation, without coming under the cognizance of courts of justice, or into the balance of statistics.

The converse is equally true ; that certain actions or tendencies, which in one age have been regarded as absolute proofs of virtue, afford no proof whatever of a real general improvement in mankind ; such are the foundation of monasteries, donations to the clergy, numerous masses, prayers, sermons, &c. &c.

The task of observing and of judging are, indeed, far more easy, when directed solely to these dark or bright spots of social life, and when those who dwell in the more level regions are altogether disregarded. I, on the contrary, consider the opinions, feelings, and actions of this enormous majority as completely decisive. If, then, we put aside criminals, we cannot doubt that the great bulk of the community have gained in morality, when we consider how much an intolerant theology, a shallow philosophy, and coarse manners have lost, and are daily losing, ground.

For myself, I see the development of the highest morality in the progress of intelligence and of legislation on such subjects as pauperism, slavery, corporations, monopolies, trade, manufactures, education, &c. What is thought and done on these matters gives to a people a solid and permanent existence, a consistent career : here lie the germs and the fruits of life and of death. If these most important changes be enlightened by the sun of truth and humanity, some reflected light will fall on the dark regions of penal law.

If we compare the mass and the worth of all

that is sound in England, with the mass and the vileness of all that is unsound, the former appears in a state of much more vigorous and rapid increase than the latter. I trust, therefore, that the knell which some are so fond of ringing in our ears will be but a warning call to double solicitude and double zeal for improvement.

LETTER XLI.

Kensington Gardens—Travellers—Anecdotes of Burckhardt—
Prusssia—Personages of the Old Testament.

London, Friday, June 19th, 1835.

I BROKE off my last letter with the information
that I should dine at Kensington on the 17th of
June. The weather being favourable, I drove
out early, and walked about in the garden,
park, or wood—for any of these names may be
applied to it. The large oaks, beeches, elms,
horse and sweet chestnuts, are nevertheless its
chief ornament; and the sheep stroll about on
the green turf as if they were in Paradise. There
is a particular charm in the circumstance that the
London Parks are not (like our Thiergarten)
exclusively devoted to human beings, and quite
without animals. Here, on the contrary, cows,
horses, and sheep share the rights and enjoyments of their masters.

The company consisted of nine persons, among
whom was Mr. Waddington, author of a work on
Ecclesiastical History, who had been at Jerusa-
lem; and Mr. Davison, who had visited India,
Egypt, and Mexico, and intended to go to Tim-
buctoo, in order to proceed from that place either
to the Cape or to Egypt. He entertains the
hope of meeting with a civilized people in the

M 3

centre of Africa. On my objecting that such a people must long since have advanced to the coast, he replied, that the ancient Egyptians were not a wandering people. But who knows from what distance they came before they reached the Mediterranean, and whether there is not more truth in the stories of the triumphs of Sesostris than we are generally disposed to believe? Among other things, Mr. Davison related two anecdotes of Burckhardt. As I do not know whether they have ever yet been published, I will repeat them.

Burckhardt, after having had an audience of the Pasha of Egypt, was called back, and the Pasha said to him—" You speak Arabic with too much purity to have learned it merely by conversation. You are a German, or an Englishman, and are travelling about to write a book; say at least in it, that you did not succeed in deceiving one native of the East. You have learned everything very perfectly, but I discovered you by your feet; they are not those of an Arab, they have long been cramped in shoes."

On the road to Mecca provisions are often scarce, and Burckhardt contrived, very dexterously, to put some bread, which had been left, into his sleeve. Upon this a Turk said to him, " Now I have found you out! You are a Christian dog; you cannot trust to Providence for a single day, and therefore you have stolen the bread."

The accounts of the learned travellers entertained the company much; but at last, from modest listening, I nearly fell into useless talking; or, what is worse, into a quarrel.

One of the gentlemen present, a German into the bargain had the boldness to affirm that "Everything that has been done in Prussia was done with English money:" I added—"And with Prussian blood." On which a short but rather keen discussion ensued.

We then fell upon the subject of Hebrew, and the same person maintained that all the personages of the Old Testament were *canaille,* and would be hanged if they were alive now. I said that I could not make out why Abraham, Job, or Solomon should be hanged. "To understand that, you must read the Bible." "I have read it, and perhaps more thoroughly than you,"—&c., &c.

LETTER XLII.

Buckingham House—Dinner at Mr. Murray's—Sir Walter Scott —Cobbett— Hunt— Demagogues — Lord Brougham — Mr. O'Connell—Prospects of England.

London, June 20th, 1835.

YESTERDAY, in company with Mr. D——, and several other persons, I visited Buckingham House, the king's new palace, in St. James's Park. Many objections might be made to the arrangement and proportions of the exterior, though its extent, and the colonnade, give it a certain air of grandeur.

But what shall I say of the interior? I never saw anything that might be pronounced a more total failure, in every respect. It is said, indeed, that, spite of the immense sums which have been expended, the king is so ill-satisfied with the result, that he has no mind to take up his residence in it' when the unhappy edifice shall be finished. ᵢ This reluctance appears to me very natural. For my own part, I would not live in it rent-free; I should vex myself all the day long with the fantastic mixture of every style of architecture and decoration—the absence of all pure taste—the total want of feeling of measure and proportion. Even the great entrance-hall does not answer its object, because the principal staircase is on one side, and an immense space, scarcely lighted, seems to extend before you as you enter, to no purpose whatever. The grand apartments of the principal story are adorned with pillars; but what kind of pillars? Partly red, like raw sausages; partly blue, like starch— bad imitations of marbles which nobody ever saw, standing upon blocks which art rejects, to support nobody knows what. Then, in the next apartment (in defiance of keeping), no pillars, but pilasters; then pilasters without base or capital; and then with a capital, and with the base preposterously cut away.

In the same apartment, fragments of Egypt, Greece, Etruria, Rome, and the Middle Ages, all confusedly mingled together; the doors, windows, and chimney-pieces, in such incorrect proportions, that even the most unpractised eye must be offended. The spaces unskilfully divided, cut up, insulated; the doors sometimes in the centre, sometimes in the corner—nay, in one room there are three doors of different height and breadth; over the doors, in some apartments, bas-reliefs and sculptures, in which pygmies and Brobdignagians are huddled together — people from two to six feet high living in admirable harmony. The smaller figures have such miserable spider legs and arms, that one would fancy they had been starved in a time of scarcity, and were come to the king's palace to fatten.

The picture gallery is highly spoken of. I allow it is large, and the Gothic branches, depending from the half-vaulted ceilings, produce a certain effect. On the other hand, this imitation of Henry the Seventh's chapel is out of its place here, where the doors and windows belong to other times and other nations. These doors and windows, again, are in no proper proportion to the whole; the immensely high wall cannot be hung with paintings; and the light, coming from above on two sides, is false, insufficient, and, moreover, broken by the architectural decorations.

This palace, therefore, stands as a very dear proof that wealth, without knowledge of art and taste, cannot effect so much as moderate means aided by knowledge and sound judgment. Of what use, then, is it? The best thing that could happen would be, if Aladdin, with his magic lamp, would come and transport it into an African desert. Then might travellers go in pilgrimage to it, and learned men at home might puzzle their brains over their descriptions and drawings; wondering in what a curious state of civilization and taste the unknown people, who built in such a style, must have lived! and how such deviations from all rule were to be explained! In the disputations that would arise, the people would be, if not justified, at least excused, and their liberal grants of money would be urged as extremely meritorious; but the king, and, above all, the architect, would be found guilty of a violation of all rules of art and of sense.

June 20th.

I dined with Mr. Murray, the eminent book-seller, from whom I have received great kindness and attention. I met Mrs. A——; the wife, the daughter and son of Mr. Charles Kemble, the latter of whom is thoroughly versed in the German language; his sister I have already mentioned as a distinguished singer; Mr. Milman, the reviewer of my 'Hohenstaufen,' &c. I sat between Mrs. Murray and another lady of agreeable manners. We found that her mother and mine were both of French extraction, and this formed a sort of ground of acquaintance. She entirely declined an English origin, and said, " I am a Scotchwoman." This pointed assertion of the national difference might have suggested many observations; but I was like Holberg's prating barber,—I fell again into the hundred-times repeated subject of Mary Stuart and Elizabeth. The transition from this to Sir Walter Scott was easy. I observed how much he was read in Germany, and that the pure morality of his works made them more congenial to our tastes than those of Byron, who, spite of his genius, has too much of the diabolical and the painful. From Scott's ' Abbot,' I said, we obtained a more correct knowledge of Mary's character, than from all the works of her *un*-historical advocates.

The conversation was going on, on this subject, when Mr. Murray, who probably had heard a part of it, rose, came to me, and said in a whisper, " Do you know who your neighbour is ? "—" No." —" It is the daughter of Sir Walter Scott."

I can hardly describe to you what an impression this unexpected intelligence made upon me. It was not fear lest I had said anything disagreeable —not satisfaction at having said anything flattering; nothing of this kind passed through my

mind. I scarcely know why, I dwelt on the
one idea—Walter Scott is dead. I felt only the
grief of the daughter at having lost such a father;
—her sorrow at hearing him speak only in his
works—of hearing from strangers from a distant
land a faint echo of her own feelings. I am
not ashamed to confess that I found it difficult to
suppress an emotion which was entirely out of
place in a cheerful company, and would probably
have been the most distressing to her to whom I
could the least have endured to give the slightest
pain.

         *   *   *   *

Cobbett has followed his quasi-colleague, Hunt.
Their opinions and modes of thinking, so far
from acquiring any ascendancy, might be made
to serve as a test to the House of Commons for
regarding things from a point of view, which
(in the usual course of civilization) self-raised
men never reach, or to whom it never becomes
natural. These men thought, lived, felt, like
plebeians, and therefore found an echo in the
people;—and it would have been more rational
to investigate the causes of this, than to make
it a subject of lamentation. Instead of wasting
their time in fruitless abuse, people would then
discover means of redressing real evils, of showing the groundlessness of false complaints, and
of exhibiting absurdities in all their nakedness.
If there be any individuals who think to turn the
demagogical heritage of these men to account,
they will probably find themselves mistaken.
The spirit of resistance to power, which grows
with rank luxuriance on the rough uncultured soil

of the people, has a native life, which, when trained and pruned, bears the noblest fruit,—such, for instance, as heroic devotion to country.   On the other hand, the revolutionary tendency which is nurtured in the closet, which borrows all its force from the annihilation of the positive, and thinks to lead nations captive with a few phrases, is shallow in its origin, presumptuous in its course, destructive in its results.   Popular life is far too rich, varied, earnest, and vivid, to be long chained to the dry bones of a superficial system.   Their sorrows and their joys are not to be learned from the political herbariums of system-mongers; and, when once it comes to blows, there are thoughts and feelings in motion that are not dreamt of in the philosophy of these political pedagogues.

Even the popular talent of so distinguished a mind as Brougham's wears itself out, because it sometimes trusts more to rhetoric than to truth. O'Connell, on the other hand, whenever his powers fail him, lays himself down on the soil of his injured country, and rises, like a new Antæus, to fresh struggles.   This is the secret of his strength; and it extends as far as he has reason on his side.   Hence, when he proposed the Repeal of the Union, his power vanished with the justice of his cause, and he was driven out of the field by Mr. Spring Rice, backed by a large majority.

While many of our continental augurs (I cannot help returning to them) see nothing here but confusion, crime, and misery, I am much more inclined to apply Ariosto's celebrated stanzas on the frankness and loyalty of the old knightly times. Peel and Russell, who have mutually unseated each other in the lists, now unite in the new municipal reforms; and a majority of members combine to carry one of the most important measures, without mingling any passion or party rancour in these instructive and necessary discussions. Let the great prophet of Berlin then do the like, and spare his Jeremiades for another time. If he says, that time may come;—I reply, that he knows no more of the future than others who persist in applying a French measure to English affairs.

If he must prophesy, let him do it boldly for Prussia. Let him have the courage to condemn the spirit which has been our fosterer and our deliverer, which has given us a name and glory among the nations.

I write the same things for ever: but are not the same reflexions for ever forced upon me?

LETTER XLIII.

Saturday, June 21*st*, 1835.

In the first place, my hearty good wishes for your
journey to Swinemünde, which was fixed for. to-
day. I hope the weather may be as bright, or
rather more so, than it is here; for even on the
brightest day in England there is no clear view
of the distance;—a veil of mist spreads itself over
everything, so that only the nearest objects present a distinct and sharp outline. In Italy there
is often a mist, but it is rose-coloured, or deep
blue, and plays through the whole chromatic
scale of colour. The English mist persists in its
uniform gray. So it was yesterday.

Having done my work, I went with Mr. M——
(who had already prepared another pleasure for
me) and his wife and daughter, to Greenwich,
which is six English miles from London; and
yet in London, or a continuation of it; for the
streets and houses extend thither in an unbroken
line, and at night the numberless shops were as
brilliantly illuminated as in the centre of the

capital. One always feels inclined to doubt the possibility of such an immense mass of human beings living together, and finding food within so small a space. London is certainly the Omphalos, or centre of the earth, no less than Delphi was that of the Hellenic nations. From no place do so many veins and arteries diverge in all direc_tions; a continental system attempting to stop this circulation would be as absurd as (in our days) the old English navigation law, which claims a monopoly of life and motion.

The hospital, or rather palace, for old seamen, at Greenwich, was probably intended to surpass Louis XIV.'s Hôtel des Invalides. It certainly does surpass St. James's Palace and Bucking-ham House. Its site on the Thames is happily chosen, to recall to its inmates the activity and excitement of their earlier years. Such an insti-tution cannot, however, be justified by the laws of utility. A crown given to the invalid returning to his own home goes farther than a pound sterling in such a magnificent edifice. But the nation which erected it may say, 'If I like to spend my money thus, what is that to you?' *Exegi monumentum!*

The paintings of storms at sea and of naval battles, and the portraits and statues of naval heroes, are a record of gallant deeds, a school of history, and an incitement to heroic imitation, though they do not afford much proof of a high cultivation of art.

From my place at table, I looked down the Thames and saw the ships coming up with the tide and a fair wind, with all their sails set, like black and white eagles, while the dragon-tailed steamers hurried roaring past them. The company consisted of several gentlemen and ladies, and I should have felt myself quite at home, had I been able to follow all the rapid turns of conversation. A calculation was made, that in the same time in which an Italian speaks ten, a German twelve, and a Frenchman fifteen words, an Englishman utters, or rather does not utter, but slips out, with elisions and abbreviations, twenty-five. My health was drunk in a very friendly manner: and now I was to make a speech. I felt no want of matter, thoughts and feelings (for do I not send you a treatise every day?)—but in what language was I to speak? My English would have been quite too bad, and German would have been unintelligible to many of my hearers; so I contented myself with drinking 'Long life to Old England.' *Esto perpetua!*

I went home in the evening with Mr. M——, and we stayed talking till midnight, partly about the past events and future prospects of England, partly about the state of civilization and the character of Germany and Prussia.

I should not have a drop of historical blood in my veins, if I did not sympathize in the melancholy with which many look back into past times; if I could not understand the feeling which urges so many a noble mind to try to retain unchanged the institutions which supported the power, and increased the glory of England. But flowers fade, trees decay, buildings fall into ruins, and nations disappear from the earth. Where, then, lies the sustaining and revivifying power? Not in the unchanging, the uniform, the motionless; these are rather the signs and characteristics of death,—nay, even death is but another name for change and re-creation: and thus, for the continuance of vegetable life, we require fresh seed; for the maintenance of the strongest edifice, constant inspection and repair.

The individual man must die; but he dies and leaves his blessing to his posterity. He knows that they will not be like him in everything; far from regretting this, he wishes that they should avoid his faults and his weaknesses.

But all this is trivial. I meant to say something very different. I deny the necessity for the utter decay and fall of nations. It is said, nations consist of individuals—all individuals must die—therefore all nations must die.—The analogy and the inference are false. Because all plants die, does it follow that all the genera and species must die out? Does not a power of eternal regeneration lie in the great whole?

No nation has ever fallen but by its own vices and crimes; and the belief in an eternal existence—the duty of maintaining that existence—is the first article of a national creed, the first rule of a national law.—*Nil desperandum.* This firm persuasion rests not on selfish presumption; on the contrary, it is inseparably connected with the recognition of the existence and the permanence of others, and the utter rejection of all lust of conquest and of overthrow. According to the common notions, Athens was doomed to death when the Persian, and Rome when the Gaul, were within her walls ; Prussia, in the Seven Years' War and the war with France ; Spain and Russia, when Napoleon entered Madrid and Moscow. But it was not so.

There indisputably do exist incurable causes of ruin. But even then the laurel may overshadow the grave, as well as the cypress—witness Car-thage and Numantia.

Our times are more prolific in the means of prolonging national life than any preceding ones. First, in material means,—in the greater know-ledge and improvement of the earth and its pro-ductions, in more active intercourse and more liberal mutual assistance. Secondly, financial and military,—in the more equal division of all things, and the more equitable claims on pro-perty and life. Thirdly, legal and political,—in the abolition of slavery, villenage, and the ex-clusive tyranny of any individual or any class. Fourthly, moral and religious,—in the stream of eternal life, which may and should pervade, sanc-tify, and bless, every relation of human life from the fount of genuine Christianity. Therefore, again I say—*Nil desperandum!*

Monday, June 26, 1835.

Yesterday I wandered into the Regent's Park, and saw how the people amuse themselves on a Sunday. Of eating, drinking, singing, music, dancing, not a trace—they walk up and down, and lie on the grass, which is now growing sear and yellow. A number of pretty children ; but not in those joyous groups or graceful attitudes with which the little Parisians so often delighted themselves and me in the Tuileries.

I dined with the Chancellor of the Exchequer. My little essay on our municipal system gave occasion to a discussion on this subject, and the conversation on finance, taxation, free trade, commercial unions, &c., which lasted the whole time of dinner, was extremely interesting. I acquire some information in every society, and I am often delighted to have an opportunity of representing our fatherland in a light as true as it is favourable.

Firmly as I am resolved not to report one word of the private conversations of individuals, which could be in the slightest degree disagreeable to them, I trust it is no gossip, *à la* ——, to repeat a *contraband* story or two from an authentic source.

A few days ago a lady sent ten guineas, and a merchant 3000*l.*, to the Exchequer, with the acknowledgment that they had formerly defrauded the revenue to that amount.

The Custom-House officers received information that a great number of Swiss watches were smuggled in certain bales of goods, on board a certain ship. All search, however, was fruitless; at length it was discovered that holes were cut in the thick packing cases, and the watches hidden in them.

A ship discharged slate as ballast; in the slate

Florentine mosaic was most dexterously concealed.

People are right, in one view, to look upon smugglers as criminals; in another, they are the great promoters of moderate duties and free trade. On this ground, they deserve more praise than many German liberals, who, in spite of all their pretended superiority, cling to old prejudices and petty interests, deny the advantages of the German commercial league, and give the lie to the very opinions they trumpet forth.

Mr. —— told me that Monsieur —— is just arrived from Germany, and gave him a great deal of information about that country. According to him, not only has the old hatred to France entirely disappeared, but the Germans now look to her for succour and for wisdom. Of the boasted German nationality he could not discover a trace —and so forth.

It is true, and no less honourable than true, that blind, passionate, national antipathy has been softened by the blessed influence of peace; but if France were to show any desire to enter on her old career, the same aggressions would excite the same resistance. Mr. —— has, perhaps, fallen in with some persons who, like B—— and H——, regard patriotism as a prejudice; and in bad French describe to him Germany—with which they have nothing in common—as a ripe plum, which the French may shake down and eat at their pleasure. What would these magnanimous cosmopolitans say, if one were to try to prove to them, from the gossip of a few Carlists,

that France was longing for Cossacks and Bash-
kirs to deliver her from a state of anarchy, and
restore the reign of law and order? Has not
history, then, sufficiently proved that a foreign
people can no more confer freedom, than a
dastardly people can inspire courage, or a licen-
tious purity? Centuries of experience ought to
teach the French that, out of their own country,
they have never succeeded in permanently attaching hearts or heads; and that their powers and
exertions, when applied at home, have brought
forth far more lasting and honourable results.
Whenever the moment shall arrive in which they
will consent to relinquish the persuasion that
they are the predestined guardians and governors of other nations, full justice will be done
to their admirable qualities; and when they
cease to excite anxiety and dread, they will cease
to inspire secret aversion. Germany and central
Europe have equal reason to reject the selfish
philanthropy of France, and the autocratic domination of Russia.

" Frederic II. of Prussia," writes Lord Hynd-
ford, in the year 1741, " is a madman, who will ruin
himself in a few months. He does not understand that he is nothing, unless by attaching
himself to others; he forgets that the House of
Brandenburg can play but a second or a third
part, and he madly insists on undertaking a
first."

So for centuries thought, spoke, and acted the
northern and western neighbours of Germany.
Germany was the field of blood on which Sweden

and France haughtily cast lots for the spoil of
the greatest of empires; and, after Sweden sank
into insignificance, the Russian and French diplomatists seated themselves on the Imperial throne
at Rastadt, and played roulette for electorates,
archbishoprics, bishoprics, dukedoms, and prin-
cipalities. Germany deserved her chastisement
for having kissed the dust of the feet of her
southern prefects and her northern satraps.

If the French could so far master their vanity and their lust of conquest as to regard all
territorial extension of their power as injurious,
they would immediately conciliate all minds, and
might regard Germany as their rampart against
the aggressions of Russia. But how is it possible that Prussia, for example, can come to
any cordial understanding with them so long
as they daily maintain that the left bank of the
Rhine is their right and their inheritance? A
thousand years are in the sight of these gods no
more than a day; and love of country (which they
justly boast in themselves) they treat as a folly
which must give way before the power of a few
phrases about natural boundaries. No neighbour-
ing nation has the least to dread from the Germans
as an *aggressive* people. It never does, and never
can, occur to them to make conquest of Russian
or French territory. The continuance of oppressive burthens, the waste of means and energies,
attendant on war establishments and standing
armies, is therefore mainly attributable to France
and Russia. They, secure in their position, might
without the slightest danger set an example which

the rest of Europe would gladly follow.   Such an example would afford the best proof of honest and pacific intentions.

The old talk about natural friends and natural enemies generally refers to petty considerations, and implies vulgar opinions and sentiments.   A loftier wisdom and a truer charity teach that *all* nations are natural friends; that all have reason to rejoice in every step in the career of human improvement, on whatever soil it be set.   But old formulas have been succeeded by new ones,—for every age has its political partialities and prejudices, according to which every thing is judged, and which are regarded as unerring pole-stars. Now we have barriers of rank, equality, constitutions, absolutism, sovereignty of the people, &c. In every one of these ideas lies an element of what is true and venerable; but as soon as we regard what is individual and conditional as absolute;—as soon as we magnify the limited beyond its actual size,—all truth and beauty vanish, and we see only caricature and deformity.

Were it not for the omnipotence of phrases and of prejudices, how, for example, were it possible that people could believe that the question of legitimacy—that is of legal succession—involves the whole weal or woe of Spain?   Undoubtedly a firmly settled law of succession is one of the greatest advantages of the monarchical form of government; and he who excites or rather forces doubt upon it, throws a firebrand into a house, already tottering beneath the weight of time and decay.   But these doubts may be ended nobly:

Constantine and Nicholas will have a brilliant
page in history, when compared with Pedro and
Miguel, Carlos and Isabella. The morbid matter
in Spain is of extremely various kinds; and behind
the names which are used as war cries, there lie
hid, on either side, matters of a very different
nature, and contradictions too monstrous for the
intervention or non-intervention of foreigners,
—that algebraic equation of politics,—easily to
solve, or to reduce to equal and pure quantities.

European politics, from the fortunate absence
of a direction forced upon them by necessity, have
fallen into the delays and entanglements of
diplomacy. And yet, if we put aside the interests
of the mere moment, there is but one grand task
to achieve: namely, to take care that France and
Russia neither come to the shock of open hostility, nor unite for the subjugation of Europe.
This is the mighty, and almost superhuman task
of central Europe. If, on the contrary, any of the
other nations,—Prussia, for example,—subjected
herself, from fear or from favour, to a foreign
policy, whether French or Russian, and suffered
herself thus to be towed in their wake, she would
act a part unworthy of herself; a part which, so
long ago as 1741, Frederic II. disdained. The
true and enlarged policy of France and of Russia—
the best interests of both countries—demand that
the centre of Europe should be powerful. But
if this grand point were abandoned, it does not
follow that Germany must make such an avowal
of weakness as to cling for protection to either of
these giants; she must seek her safety from her-

self. If central Germany, Austria, and Prussia, are really united, they may resist all aggressions ; they have more to fear from their own disunion than from the union of their enemies. And even were this not the case, they have England on their side. ' England ! I hear some exclaim with scorn, England ! who consumes her strength in her own wretched broils ! who is so fallen from her ancient glory, that she regards the flatteries· of French diplomatists and journalists as her highest reward ! who outdoes France herself in the extravagance of her revolutionary opinions ! shall we trust to England for succour or for safety? What folly ! Once, indeed, Europe held fast to this anchor ; but now, thanks to French assistance and her own levity, the anchor is broken, and the cables so worn, that they would not moor a fishing-boat securely.

I by no means undertake to defend the policy of England on all points during late years ; but as little can I defend that of her accusers. States, like man and wife, sometimes get into ill-humour with each other, and vent it in mutual annoyances.

But those who are bound by a common interest, and common sympathies, should not be separated by transient disgusts. And if such were to arise between Prussia and England, a real statesman would not, like an angry woman, push things to extremity, but endeavour to restore and to consolidate the natural relations by wisdom and moderation.

If, which Heaven avert ! Russia were ever to

march an army to the Oder, or France to the Rhine, the British lion would rouse himself from his lair, and show a strength which those little dream of who think him decrepit and effete, because he did not choose to rise up, and to come and go, at their bidding!

You cry—a political letter, a tiresome letter! and I admit the charge, the more readily as I have fallen involuntarily into the course, when I should have been much better and more agreeably employed in speaking of the daughter of ———— my neighbour at table. But I can sooner find courage to attack the policy of powerful courts, than to speak out my admiration of those who are the most worthy and the least covetous of such eulogies. I will therefore confine myself to this general declaration, that English men and women please me more, the more I know them.

Wednesday, June 23rd.

The day before yesterday I dined with Mr. T. yesterday I saw the King's collection of Pictures, and went to the Haymarket Theatre. This, omitting reading, writing, and visiting, is the outline of my history. As to the first family, which is as refined as it is simple, I must repeat my former praises, if you desire a commentary on my table of contents. As to the pictures, Waagen, who is master of the subject, will at some future time make his report. It consists, almost entirely, of Flemish masters, and here are specimens of

their peculiar merits, in three different styles;—
landscape, comic scenes, and portraits. Berghem,
Vandervelde, Cuyp, Potter, Mieris, Teniers, Os-
tade, Vandyk, and Rubens, are the most remarkable; several less celebrated masters deserve
the place they hold among them. But the historical pictures of the Flemings are often tasteless
and exaggerated; their allegories cold; and their
Holy Families, portraits of their own families, or
at any rate of mere human beings. The grave
Dutchmen succeed best in drollery and caricature; the lively and passionate Italians, in calm
and serious refinement. The artistical character
of each is thus in perfect contrast to their ordinary
nature; perhaps this very contrast forms the
necessary complement of their being. I see
nothing like this in the English. Their music,
sculpture, and painting are now, as formerly,
very inferior to those of any of the nations which
have acted as leaders of the human race: yet
their Shakspeare rules supreme over every part
of the world of grief or joy. He is the universal
monarch of modern poetry, compared with whom
other poets are but lords of subordinate and
bounded territories.

At the Haymarket I saw the 'Beggars' Opera,'
which has been so long celebrated and admired.
The simple airs have indeed quite as much originality as most of the modern music that is now
so much preferred; it has considerable vivacity
and characteristic conception; but the inventive
genius is not always in perfect harmony with the
sentiments; probably because most of the me-

'lodies were old ones, and derived great part of their effect from their antiquity. The 'Beggars' Opera' is a pleasing production, but cannot be classed among the imperishable models and masterpieces of art. I have more objections to make against the story on seeing it acted than when I read it. In particular, Captain Macheath is too nearly allied to a vulgar vagabond, and has too little force or originality, to justify the dispute of the beauties for his favour. All the coarser and more overstrained characters were the best supported. The sentimental parts were as insipid as an English dish of vegetables. The singing was very much applauded, and certainly was better than that in most French vaudevilles. This is a very slender merit, and yet I cannot conscientiously give it greater praise.

As to the second piece, 'Teazing made Easy,' I must repeat my former opinion about the principal parts. Certain favourite actors, Buckstone, for example, seem to use the same action in representing very different characters. A particular manner of speaking and moving, particular gestures and noises, are resorted to so constantly by some comic actors (as in Germany), that they rather represent a class than create one of those individual pictures which we can single out from all the world. On the whole, the representation was lively and entertaining: the shrewish Mrs. Teazer (Miss Daly), and Mrs. Humby (who was the Lucy of the Beggars' Opera) as Molly Mixem, were very amusing. The mixture of tenderness and anger in the former piece; of gentility and

N 3

vulgarity, of submissiveness and impatience, in the latter, was admirably given by this lady, and not over-coloured. A place in the pit of the Haymarket costs a thaler: this price, combined with other inconveniences, would frighten even those in easy circumstances in our country; but here people have more money.

Behind me sat a lady, for such I thought the thaler entitled her to be considered. At the end of the first piece she opened a basket, took out a bottle and a glass, and offered her right-hand neighbour a bumper. The contents of it being too strong for him, and making him cough and wink his eyes, her left hand neighbour called out, "Go on, go on!" But his exhortation was of no avail; whereupon this Hebe of the Haymarket drank off the rejected liquid fire with a serene and cheerful countenance!

This dramatic interlude did not seem to excite my astonishment only, but that of the Englishmen around. Probably, therefore, it is fair to regard it as an exceptional or abnormal incident, such as are to be found in all countries.

LETTER XLIV.

English Popular Eloquence—Specimens of Speeches to Constituents—Pledges—Absence of Philosophical Principles—Debates
on Paper Currency and Ballot.

London, June 24th, 1835.

THE tone and manner which the Members of the
House of Commons adopt when speaking in their
places is in many respects different to that with
which they address their constituents. This difference would be absolutely condemned by over-
rigid critics, who denounce popular eloquence as
altogether mischievous. It certainly is not without its abuses; but still less is it entirely devoid
of utility. Occasional extravagances are immediately corrected by men of different opinions.
Neither is it so easy to decide as to the expediency
of the pledges which are demanded and given.
On the one hand, it is both natural and just that
the constituents should desire to know how the
candidate intends to vote on certain leading questions: on the other, unconditional promises on
every point would annihilate the true character of
a representative system, bring back the miseries
of the French *Cahiers* of 1789, and would, in fact,
render all deliberation, and all rectification of
errors and prejudices, impossible. Such a constant despotism of the constituents would render
the members mere machines.

As I cannot take for granted that you are acquainted with the speeches made at elections, I will send you a short abridgment of those of a few remarkable men.

[Here follows a very abridged report of speeches made at their several elections by the following members:—Mr. Abercromby, Dr. Bowring, Mr. Bulwer, Sir F. Burdett, Sir J. Campbell, Messrs. Cobbett, Grattan, Hume, Jervis, Sir Robert Inglis, Sir E. Knatchbull, Lord Mahon, Lord Morpeth, Mr. O'Connell, Mr. Spring Rice, Mr. Roebuck, Lord John Russell, Lord Sandon, and Lord Stormont. These it has been thought advisable to omit.]

But-enough of these specimens. You find in them the absurdities of certain extreme opinions; yet it is impossible not to discover some grounds and occasions even for these extremes,—not to perceive that a portion of truth lies at the bottom of them. And, after all, it is better that there should be a representative of every conceivable way of thinking in Parliament, than that an overbearing power should compress all into one form, and tinge all with one colour. No individual ventures downright to recommend either persistency, or change, in the abstract; all concede the necessity and the possibility of improvement. But the uncertainty, the doubt, the ambiguity, lies here; that every one attaches a different idea to this word improvement; every one would take his stand on a different step of the ladder. There is more danger to be apprehended from this confusion of ideas in the mass of the people, than from the glaring errors of individuals: at least, the excessive dread which the English have-of anything that looks like a theoretical system, or an absolute philosophical principle, will render it, perhaps, more difficult to devise measures and remedies applicable and acceptable to all.

The bare abstract philosophy of the French and Germans leads, it is true, to no definite end; but without science, the heaping together a quantity of detached facts and precedents serves only to increase the confusion and darkness. What is there that might not be proved in this manner, in an old and complex state of society?

But if it is not to be expected that any scientific school should arise to guide the unsteady current of opinions; if it is least of all to be desired that a narrow utilitarianism should be generally received; yet those are greatly mistaken who predict that the exasperated parties stand on the brink of a fearful revolution. As soon as they come to the discussion and decision of serious questions (with the almost single exception of church affairs, where things are smuggled into the territory of conscience and divine ordinances); as soon, I repeat, as they come to great practical questions, the majority feel the necessity of moderation and concession. They must see that a victory won on insecure ground can give to the ministry, whose rise is built upon it, no pledge for its durability. Hence the Whigs voted with the Tories against the repeal of the malt tax; and hence the important questions on the currency and the ballot were decided by a large majority. Lord J. Russell and Sir Robert Peel, with their respective adherents, far from being actuated by blind party rage, acted in concert.

Both these subjects were expounded in the

House of Commons with acuteness and solidity; especially by Mr. Poulett Thomson and Lord J. Russell. Ou both occasions I should have voted with the majority.

The idea of creating wealth by the manufacture of bank-notes,—creating it, moreover, for the sole advantage of one class, the agriculturists,—is a most preposterous one, and, in the end, could serve only to favour the debtor, to the injury of the creditor. It is only when some generous ruler surrenders a large sum, free of interest, that the receivers, those manufacturers of wealth, can conveniently divide the interest, as the profits of a bank; they may then speak very favourably of the benefits of an increased paper-currency, from their own experience.

The evils and vices of the English, as of every elective system, are not attempted to be concealed in recent discussions. It is only asserted that, in the present posture of things, no adequate remedy could be found in secrecy of suffrage; and that it would be right to wait the result of longer experience, before applying entirely new principles. If all the tenants of England were proprietors, it is not to be doubted that their votes at elections would be far more independent than they are. But whether the destruction of the aristocratical influence of great landed proprietors would be injurious, and the increase of democratical interference beneficial, is a question on which opinions and views are naturally very much divided.

LETTER XLV.

National Gallery—English Painters—Poussin, Claude, Sebastian del Piombo, Correggio—Gloomy Predictions—Weather—Blue Devils—English Travelling—Coleridge's Table Talk—Canning—The French Character——English Philosophy—Cologne.

June 25th, 1835.

My time here is so limited, and every day so fully occupied, that I am not able to see many most interesting things. Thus, I went yesterday, for the first time, to the National Gallery. It is inferior to many others in the number of pictures, but it has some of the highest class. Among these I cannot reckon, according to my feelings, the historical and scripture paintings of West and Reynolds, nor the landscapes of some English painters. A series of paintings by Hogarth confirms what we already know from the engravings, of the peculiar and witty conceptions of this master. Some of Wilkie's pictures may be placed in the same rank as the best pieces of familiar life of the Flemish school. We find Rembrandt here in a new character, namely, as a finished painter of small figures : and there is a Bacchanalian scene by Nicolas Poussin which I prefer to anything I have seen of that master.

The landscapes of Gaspar Poussin afford fresh proof of the vigour of his poetical view of nature, although his deep shadows conceal many parts worthy of being seen. Some sea-pieces, with buildings and ships, by Claude Lorraine, are perfect beyond description. What lights, what clouds and waves, what an etherial sky and atmosphere! It is only in her loveliest days that nature presents herself under such an aspect; nor has any artist but Claude known how to 'seize and immortalize this evanescent beauty.. The longer one looks at these pictures, the more striking are their truth and beauty. They are among the most finished productions I have ever seen by this artist.

. The raising of Lazarus, designed by Michael Angelo,.and painted by Sebastian del Piombo, is of the same size as Raphael's Transfiguration, and a worthy companion to it. It is a complete dramatic poem; and portrays every emotion which this miracle of the .Saviour would naturally call forth in the mind of. man,—doubt and faith, hope and thankfulness, wonder and fear. Each individual bears the stamp of his distinct character, impossible to mistake; and yet, spite of such infinite variety, a perfect unity of design and effect is preserved. And how perfect is the drawing and execution!—a.fresh proof of the greatness of Michael Angelo and of his pupil. · ·

. Two pictures by Correggio exhibited this master to me in a new and.unknown perfection. The first, Venus,. Cupid,. and Mercury, has · undoubtedly (as a near inspection shows) suffered in one part, but, seen from a proper distance, it produces.an effect almost incredible. It is not a mere painting; it is rounded like a statue : nay, it is not sculpture,—it is nature herself in her fullest truth and beauty.   The eyes appear to see; the extended arm may be grasped; the knee is really bent; the light falls full or broken on the living body; the bosom heaves with the breath. Pygmalion's miracle is here accomplished !   What scandalous declamation, some Puritans will exclaim, about an abominable naked woman ! Well, then, let us go on to the second, still more marvellous picture; for that Correggio understood how to paint flesh, how to manage chiaro'scuro, how to relieve and foreshorten the limbs, is well known and acknowledged.   In this picture we see Christ crowned with thorns ; near him is the fainting Mary, supported by her friend; on the right, a soldier; on the left, Pilate looking out from his house.   What majesty in the Christ !   Godlike power and human suffering, consolation in sorrow, confidence in the midst of pain, devotion and resignation,—all these problems and mysteries in the nature of the Redeemer are revealed and confirmed by art to the apprehensive eye.   And the Mary !   The last groan still trembles on her pale lips ; her-closed eye speaks a language more expressive, more touching, more penetrating, than a thousand open ones.   It is only by degrees that one can turn from this sentiment, which carries one beyond all outward things, to the consideration and estimation of the individual parts, and the admiration of the technical perfections. The body of Christ is neither soft nor hard,—equally removed from both these faults. And the singularly

beautiful hands! the crown of thorns, so finely
painted, that this alone would secure admiration
to any other artist! Whoever thinks that Correggio could not represent corporeal beauty without affectation, that he never understood the spiritual, nor got beyond a cold brilliancy of the
surface, should see these pictures, and convince
himself that Correggio might, as compared with
the painter of the Farnesina as well as of the
Transfiguration, justly say, "Anch' io son pittore!"
The Christ, the Mary, and the conception and
treatment of the subject, may justly be reckoned
among the masterpieces of any artist or of any
school. How much I wish that Tieck, the most
enlightened judge and enthusiastic admirer of
Correggio, had seen these pictures! ·He would
not only have found his assertions confirmed, but
his most daring and secret anticipations fulfilled.
If you think that my old predilection for this
master (see my 'Italian Letters' and the 'Wilhel-
mine') breaks out again here, wait till Waagen,
who is of the same opinion about this miraculous
work, can give his account, and confirm my opinion.

I dined yesterday with Mr. L. He is a Tory,
thinks the prospects of England more gloomy than
I do, and fears an approaching revolution. On a
difference of opinion as to the proper meaning of
this word, I proposed to adopt,—England is in a
state of revolution when the 3 per cent. stocks
stand at 30. He promised to pay me the expenses of another journey to England, if I find
the funds higher at my return. This proposal

was, of course, not accepted.　Complaints, I added, often pass in our days for proofs of sagacity or of benevolence; contentment, for stupidity and indifference.　An Englishman, who had returned six months ago, after an absence of many years, remarked, that he sought everywhere for the distress, poverty, and disorder, which are so much complained of, but had not yet been able to find them.　So it is with me.

Friday, June 26th.

Had I a day of rest yesterday or not?　I was at work and in motion the whole day; and the only difference was, that, for the first time for many weeks, I did not spend the evening in company, but went to bed at ten o'clock.　Body and soul seemed to long all the more for this, certainly rather trifling, refreshment, because, for the last three days, storm, rain, and cold have prevailed to such a degree, that the warmest winter-clothing was not too warm, and in any room without a fire the breath was visible.

To-day Nature seems to repose.　This unseasonable season has sometimes thrown me into fits of unseasonable melancholy; I have thought how ill it must fare with you in Swinemünde with such weather.　Your object appeared to me defeated there, and mine no less here; for with all my zeal and industry I can no more exhaust the treasures of the past and the present, than I can drink up the sea.　My spoils no longer appeared to me so rich; on the contrary, I was ashamed of my project of laying anything so superficial and insignificant before the world. In about forty days I must leave London, and, independent of all literary avocations, I want more time than that merely to see what is in every guide-book. Nor is the time allotted for seeing the face of the country less insufficient, and whatever I add to the one must be taken from the other. A longer absence from home is forbidden by the wish of a speedy return, the exhaustion of pecuniary resources, the duty of giving lectures, and the expediency of printing my remarks on the present state of England as soon as possible. Every day gives birth to new events and new circumstances, and it is quite impossible to find anything final and conclusive in these regions. Then I thought of the two sides of English travelling, "outside and inside," and each, for different but sufficient reasons, pleased me as little as the other.

Such was yesterday;—to-day the sun shines, and though I shall not rashly tune my lyre for a hymn, I shall adhere to my intentions, and meditate upon the improvements and accommodations of travelling in Great Britain.

In the year 1678 an agreement was entered into, that a coach with six horses should perform the journey from Edinburgh to Glasgow, a distance of forty-four English miles, in three days! In the middle of the last century the mail-coach was a day and a half in performing the same journey. Now, it is done in four and a half or five hours! Up to the year 1763 one post-coach went once a month from London to Edinburgh, and was twelve or fourteen days on the road;

now, there are a vast number of coaches and steam-boats, the former of which perform the journey in from forty-five to forty-eight hours *.

When we consider how alterations of this kind gradually extend over the whole world, and what an incalculable mass of labour and time is thus spared; when we think how this fact is connected with innumerable others equally advantageous, we are justified in regarding these advances as highly important, and can hardly wish back again the good old times, at least as far as travelling is concerned.   But if this point is conceded to me, I can go on from it to other points, such as the progress which must ensue upon more extended and yet closer intercourse, and more easy communication; and so, from improved roads, carriages, inns, eating, drinking, &c., to the increased number of travellers, the more varied objects, the physical advantages, the intellectual cultivation, &c. &c.

Saturday, June 27th, 1835.

Appearances are deceitful: yesterday, after a sunny morning, came cold, fog, storm, and rain, worse than for the last three days,—such weather, in short, as I never saw at this season.   All plans for visits, parties, theatre, &c., lost their attraction : I was thankful to wade to the State-Paper Office, and then to the Athenæum.

At the latter place I took up Coleridge's 'Table Talk,' and was delighted with the varied, interesting remarks of this extraordinary man.   There is an annoying, vexatious way of lying in wait for

* M'Culloch's ' Dictionary,'—Roads.

and seizing every word a man speaks; but the
spoken word of a man of genius is not less precious
than the written, and it is a loss when the former
is not treasured up by attentive hearers, and
transformed into the latter. I will give a sentence or two of very different sorts, as a specimen,
accompanied perhaps with marginal glosses.

" Canning kindled such a flashing fire around
the government, that one could not see the ruins
of the edifice through it."

Very true. He played the part of an advocate
as a means of warding off attacks. Very different
from this part is that of the historian, who has to
divide his sympathy equally between opposite
sides, and represent each with equal interest.
The business of the statesman is action, and his
prime qualities are calm, undisturbed reflection,
and acute perception of existing wants. Canning
understood this well as soon as he thought the
right moment for action was come.

" The French are like grains of gunpowder;
each one, separately, is dirty and despicable, but
put them together and they become formidable."

The copy at the Athenæum was marked with
great *nota benes* of English approbation. Yet
the latter half of the sentence alone is true, and
the well-known expression of " swinish multitude "
is just as applicable to certain classes in England.
And if we speak of the French who are above
the common herd, it is far nearer the truth to say
that they are generally brilliant and amiable. I
should rather liken 'them to quicksilver, which,
on a level surface, moves in every direction in a

thousand sparkling and apparently independent globules. As soon, however, as the level line of the surface is from any cause in the least degree altered (for example, by foreign hostility), the severed drops rush together, and he who fancied he could guide or govern them is suddenly borne down by their resistless weight. For this reason it is the grand policy of foreign powers to prevent such unions, or, at any rate, not to give occasion to them.

" Every man is either a born Aristotelian, or a born Platonist. I do not believe that the one can ever be transformed into the other."

This contrast is certainly more frequent than is generally thought, and betrays itself on innumerable points, even in those who have never attained to any philosophical consciousness of the difference ; but I deny that it is so absolute that no union of the two can be imagined, or ought to be attempted. The mere superficial mixture and patchwork, which is the method of the greater number of Eclectics, is indeed one that leads to error, or to nothing ; but it cannot be true that all the powers and operations of the mind should tend to nothing else but a hostile contraposition and mutual confutation. It were far more appropriate to compare Aristotle and Plato to body and soul, the independence and the union of which together constitute life, and the separation would be death and annihilation if we had not the hope of a resurrection. My attention has been strongly directed towards the colossal greatness of these two men, who, though dead for centuries, yet live, by an article in the 'London Review,' in which a shallow utilitarianism arrogantly seats itself on the throne of philosophy, and throws around itself a royal mantle of patchwork. No turning of phrases, or shuffling of words, are sufficient to conceal the original barrenness of this system, or to entitle its professors to intrude even into the vestibules of philosophy. The English sentimental philosophy was defective on the side of philosophical perception. But what a nobleness of thought does that display in comparison with this system, which, spite of all attempts to deny it, is at last merely selfish ! If, in the former, thought and feeling were not accurately balanced, in the latter, thought and feeling are equally dried up under the domination of self-will and caprice; and this philosophical hay is proffered as the last result of all ages, in comparison with which the flower-gardens of Plato and the forests of Aristotle were unmeaning child's-play and pedantic obscurity. If this philosophy were ever to take root in the heads and hearts of the great body of Englishmen, I should think that a more dangerous revolution than any which is dreaded.

I will give you the marginal note to the fourth passage from the 'Table Talk.' The good city of Cologne has for many years been so loud in its own praises, or has been the object of so much poetical or unpoetical flattery, that it will be horrified when it learns what feelings took possession of Coleridge within its walls. He writes as follows :—

" In Cöln, that town of monks and bones,
  And pavements fang'd with murderous stones,
  And rags, and hags, and hideous wenches,
  I counted two and seventy stenches,
  All well defined and genuine stinks!
  Ye Nymphs that reign o'er sewers and sinks,
  The river Rhine, it is well known,
  Doth wash the city of Cologne;
  But tell me, Nymphs, what power divine
  Shall henceforth wash the river Rhine ? "

LETTER XLVI.

Visits—Bentham—Originality—Doctrine of Utility—Locke—
  Haymarket Theatre—' The Queen's Champion'—Sheridan's
  Rivals—Mr. K.—Hamlet.

Sunday, June 28th, 1835.

I CAN very well imagine the situation of a foreigner who lives here entirely without society,
and is consequently miserable and out of humour
with the country; but I certainly cannot sympathize in it: on the contrary, it is impossible
for me to avail myself of all the kind and polite
invitations I receive. Yesterday evening I was
invited by both B—— and D——; to-day by
K—— and M——; to-morrow by Lord E——
and Earl M-——. Instructive and agreeable as
this variety is, both body and mind want repose;
and from time to time it is a duty and a necessity
to comply with their demands. Yesterday, after
I had travelled from Petersburg to Paris and
Madrid in the State-Paper Office, I went to call
on Mrs. A——, and presented to her a copy of
my letters from Paris in the year 1830.

The conversation fell on Bentham and Locke.
The former was of opinion that the study of ancient philosophy was injurious to originality, and
that the world stood in need of something new
and different. I think, on the contrary, that he

whose originality, so far from being destroyed, is not invigorated, by the near contemplation of great spirits, has in reality none, or so little that it is not worth talking about. There is no greater felicity for a mind, whether more or less vigorous, than to come in contact with superior natures. It is not placing myself far from the light of others that will make me a sun. The real advantage of a philosophical life does not consist in the gratification of vanity and self-complacency, but in a constant and intimate intercourse with the foremost spirits of all ages, and in the appropriation of the revelations of their genius; while in the course of ordinary life we are often condemned to the society of the dull and empty. When I was in Rome I heard some beardless German artists say, they did not go into the Stanze and the Sistine Chapel for fear of injuring their originality; and certainly they produced something so new and original that it seemed to have been painted before art had been cultivated at all.

Servile imitation is never of any value, and every age calls for new manifestations of thought and genius: this novelty, however, must not be a rude beginning, or a mere germ; but the blossoms which burst forth in their own peculiar freshness and beauty from the branches of the ancient stem of all intellectual culture. Often what is enounced as new is only the forgotten and unknown, or the old, turned and altered—for the worse. The doctrine of utility, as Thrasymachus expounds it, in Plato's Republic, has a very different force and freshness from the modern growth of shops and exchanges. Epicurus's system is indeed rather an abortive philosophical essay than a philosophy; yet, viewed in connexion with the whole current of philosophical history, it is intelligible and natural: now, presumptuously put forth under the name of philosophy, it appears as absurd as pernicious. No doubt, by a perversion of language, good and useful, philanthropical and self-loving, &c. &c., may be used as synonymous. But these are generally sophistical arts, and a smuggling of evil under false colours. And to what end should the chaos of language be brought back, after the philosophical labours of thousands of years have established and defined the signification and value of words? He who does not know and understand the results of these labours, lives, to the end of his life, without penetrating within the circle of philosophy. When Plato taught that, in each individual virtue the sum of all virtues lies hidden, this endeavour to synonymize and equalize was part of his office as a philosopher. He knew well how the particular stands related to the general, and blends with it. But when, in our days, an Englishman maintains that it is absurd to make any distinction between the understanding and the reason, his apprehension and knowledge may fit him to appear with credit in the halls or marts of trade, but certainly not in the courts of philosophy.

I sometimes hear people complain here, that Locke is not honoured as he deserves in Ger-

many—a reproach which appears to me unfounded.
We do justice to his character and his principles;
but we certainly do not revere him as the father
of all modern philosophy. Even the title of his
book, 'On the Human Understanding,' shows
that he apprehended and expounded only one
side of philosophy. Of this side, however, Aristotle is a much more powerful and comprehensive
expositor; and Leibnitz and Spinoza will ever
occupy a higher place as profound thinkers.

Did not the English themselves feel the un-
satisfactoriness of Locke's philosophy? And did
they not find something more living in the doctrine of immediate sensation; or seek, like Hume,
to scepticize away the whole fabric of empiricism,
which some deemed so immutably established?
Doubt is certainly not an end, for it is nothing
positive; but the eighteenth century affords fearful proofs whither mere empiricism—which first
questions, and then denies, soul, spirit, revelation,
religion, and deity—may lead. The Germans have
undertaken and executed (not indeed without
awkwardness, pedantry, and absurdity) the vast
labour of exploring once more the whole region
of philosophical tendencies and systems, and of
placing each in a new light, and giving it a new
existence. The variety of these, and the fact that
contradictions mutually annihilate each other at
a lower point, to be re-produced in greater light
and truth at a higher, is not a defect and a
reproach, but an excellence, and a proof of the
progressive nature of science. The philosophical
structure founded by Locke cannot be regarded

as the only habitable one; and still less does
Bentham's doctrine afford all that the world requires for its regeneration in the year of our
Lord 1835.   But I think I write the same things
ten times over.   I will therefore break off, and
tell you that yesterday evening, after long deliberation on the choice, of amusements, I went
to the Haymarket Theatre, to see Sheridan's
‘ Rivals,’ which I had heard so admirably read by
Tieck.

The performance began with the ‘ Queen's
Champion,’ a piece in two acts, by Mrs. Gore:
—an anecdote or two (true or false) from the history of Marie Antoinette, cobbled together in
unhistorical connexion.

Such a fate as that of this most unhappy
Queen cannot be even mentioned without producing emotion, if people have a particle of
memory or of feeling.   But these majestic tragic
forms should be brought before us only by masters; they should be treated with a sacred awe;
their mighty and heavy sorrows, and the fearfully
profound lessons of history, should not be sold
by ounces by every small trader.   Who could
bear to see Lear, Cordelia, Hamlet, Ophelia, and
such characters and natures as these, exhibited
in two or three dramatized anecdotes, borrowed
from the gossip of a court, or the booth of a fair?
Such anecdotes are, at all events, incomplete and
out of place, when thus severed from the great
current of destiny and of history, and put forward
as weighty and independent matters.

There was much to praise and much to find

fault with in the performance of ' The Rivals.'   I
was afraid that there would be exaggeration, but
I did not find it in the entire conception, only in
particular passages.   Indeed Mr. Strickland, as
Sir Anthony Absolute, was deficient in that power
of voice, and vehemence of gesture, which are
requisite to give due importance to the character,
and the proper colour and grandeur to his anger.
One could hardly believe in the past—that is,
his youth,—neither could one exactly understand
the present.   The low comedy, indeed almost the
buffoonery, of some passages, seemed to me, too,
quite out of place.   Bob Acres (Mr. Webster)
and David (Mr. Ross) were, in many respects,
very good caricatures; but I miss, as I have before remarked, the real creative power, from the
constant sameness of the technical means.   Thus,
for example, certain servants' parts are invariably
squeaked out in the same disguised voice, which
hardly makes one laugh the first time, and, when
repeated, becomes tiresome and disagreeable.
Mrs. Malaprop (Mrs. Glover) great, in all the
three dimensions of space; Julia (Miss Taylor)
as individual as the feeble sentimentality of the
character would allow; Lydia (Mrs. Humby) the
most original and lively of all; but I should have
liked to see the pertness, caprices and fancies, a
shade more elegant and fantastic; many things
were too much like a lady's maid, or too coarsely
impertinent, and wholly devoid of poetical refinement or inspiration.   But, after all, Mrs. Humby
is, in her way, the best actress that I have seen
here, and comes nearer to Demarceaux than any

of the others to Mars; not to mention German actresses.

London, June 29.

Yesterday I paid all sorts of visits, and supped with Mr. K——, the celebrated actor. The conversation turned on the dramatic art, and on Shakspeare. He, too, thinks the former declining, and that it is hard to say how it can be revived. He thinks that Hamlet's almost incomprehensible character has more of unity and coherence if his madness is regarded as real, and not feigned; such monomania, he said, was quite consistent with understanding and deep reflection on other subjects: at all events, that it was absurd to represent him as an amiable young gentleman. I hope, some time or other, to return to this subject with him. Miss K—— sang a scene out of Handel's 'Saul' with great discrimination and feeling; and a few German songs, which transported me back to my home.

LETTER XLVII.

Difficulty of understanding England—Radicals—Tory policy—
Devonshire Election—Corporation Bill—Irish Church Bill—
Oxford—Security and Tranquillity of England.

London, June 29, 1835.

H——'s account of the celebration of Ascension
Day gave me great pleasure. Heaven grant
that all the party may meet for many years
around the board of their friendly host, and none
be absent on worse grounds than an instructive
journey to England!

And how instructive! It is perhaps easier to
form to oneself a conception of any other country,
without seeing it, than of this—our continental notions of it are in many respects so partial and false.
Few Germans, probably, have studied the history
and affairs of England so long and so attentively
as I, and yet it is only since I came here that my
knowledge has acquired certainty and consist-
ency. Newspapers like Spener's and the Staats
Zeitung are quite incompetent to diffuse just
views. Things are *not* as they represent them;
and all their conclusions are, of course, false.

I know that I may be told it is a silly arrogance in me to pretend that *my* views are the
only just ones; I do not look, however, through my
own spectacles, but through innumerable English
eyes or spectacles; and my view is not bounded

by the partiality or the hate of *one* newspaper writer, curtailed by the mutilations of censors, or warped by political projects, or by private hopes and fears. I see, and hear, and converse with persons of the most different opinions;—and are all these honest efforts to be utterly fruitless? Are they to give me no voice as opposed to those who have neither time, opportunity, inclination, nor vocation for such studies? This is not arrogance,—at least no otherwise than all individuality is, in a certain sense, arrogance.

When I called ——— an amateur in politics and in history, I was far from meaning this as a reproach, any more than I should have thought it one if he had called me an amateur of old German literature and poetry. Each of us does that which suits him, and as much as suits him, and we belong to each other, and understand each other, spite of many a discussion. And so it will be to the end of our days!

———'s letter deserves the greatest admiration for the number of good jokes, *jeux de mots*, similies, &c. I never saw a more abundant or vigorous crop of them; and I should be a great blockhead if my serious labours made me unjust to the gay manner of looking at the world, or incapable of understanding it. What I complain of is, that the general impression of England which he produces is a dark one, while I am continually more and more struck with the bright side. Many believe that her last stormy evening has set in, while I feel only the fresh morning breeze that precedes the dawn. Might

not as much danger be inferred for Germany,—
as formidable symptoms of disease be detected
in her condition,—from ——, or from G——'s
longing after atheism, which you tell me of, as
are here to be apprehended from the radicalism
of certain Benthamists?   There is no danger
from either.   One of these gentlemen, who took
a very high tone, has lately committed himself so
grossly, that he has completely overshot, or, if
you like, fallen short of, his mark.

Are not, then, (I hear you reply) even Mr.
Pattison, the Chairman of the Bank of England,
and the wealthy banker, Mr. Grote, infected with
Radicalism?   It is true they have come into Parliament as liberals; but they were the very first
to protest against the idea of refusing the Supplies.   Their whole line of conduct, and the
objects they have in view, are utterly different
from those of the Jacobins of 1792.

Sir Francis Burdett, once denounced as the
most dangerous of demagogues, voted with Canning, when the latter became the champion of
liberal measures : while Lord Grey thought himself justified in a course of continued opposition
to him.   He would not suffer himself to be led or
driven farther on the side of liberalism; and the
other day a coalition between him and the Duke
of Wellington was confidently talked of—a thing
which, a few years ago, would have been thought
impossible.   The disposition and tactics of the
French opposition generally are, to blow up all
the bridges between them and the enemy : those
of the English, on the contrary, to build them.

While it is pretended that everything here is in confusion, and is going to rack and ruin, this honourable disposition manifests itself most distinctly to all who do not confound a few bubbles and effusions of rhetorical vehemence and vanity with influential opinions and real power.

It is undoubtedly true that Wellington and Peel frankly rejected the plan of some high Tories for turning out the ministry, by the opposition of the House of Peers. This experiment indeed had been already made. They had the King and the House of Lords on their side; a new House of Commons was chosen under their influence, and even in that they were in a minority. If it is repeated towards the present ministry, they may dissolve the Parliament, and the new one will then be elected under *their* influence; so that their adversaries will only have destroyed their own work.

The defeat of Lord John Russell in Devonshire proves nothing as to the strength of parties generally: it only proves that the majority of tenants in that county, who vote under Lord Chandos's clause, are wholly dependent on Tory landlords. In consequence of a sort of re-action, the very *unconservative* proceedings at the Ipswich election are brought to light, and all the elections from that time to this have been in favour of the Whigs.

After the question of the exclusion of those who do not possess the qualifications now required in an elector is decided, the Corporation Bill will, without doubt, pass the Commons, and, I think, the Lords. It is too manifest an improvement not to command a majority of opinions in the country.

The notion, that every abuse in the general or local administration of the country is to be respected as a sacred private right, is too absurd to last.

—————— declaims against the Corporation Bill, and regards it as the climax of revolutionary degeneracy and mischief; and yet he lives quietly in a country which has possessed a completely similar municipal system for seven-and-twenty years. He regards the influence and the representation of property,—of mere material (not intellectual) qualifications,—as the true antidote to all revolutions; and forgets that the mass of property represented in the Reformed House of Commons and the reformed Corporations is infinitely greater, and consequently the influence of property stronger, than it was formerly. Either his premises, therefore, or his conclusions, are wrong.

The fate of the Irish Church Bill is more dubious than that concerning Corporations. It is complicated by the numerous personal and pecuniary interests of patrons and possessors of livings. It is also very uncertain what effect the cry " the Church is in danger " may have on English constituencies, and what colour it may give to another House of Commons. This cry has little or nothing to do with genuine Christianity. As to any application of Church property to secular uses, that is a thing not to be thought of. Are there then no circumstances which can excuse, nay justify, such an application? He who maintains, spite of numerous examples, that none such can exist, runs the risk of provoking the counter-assertion, that every application of the public revenue to ecclesiastical purposes is unjust and inadmissible. Abstract negative dogmas like these can never exhaust the circumstances of the case; and the high Tories and the Radicals, spite of their violent hostility, meet at that final point of abstraction, where Church and State lose all reciprocal and living influence. Even in the middle regions, convictions are undoubtedly at variance; but how many former ones has not Sir Robert Peel found himself compelled to abandon? I should not wonder if the proposition to pay the Catholic clergy were to come from his side, as a means of escaping the appropriation clause.

At all events the old Tory system is driven completely out of the field. Oxford, which formerly rejected Peel, now finds great cause to be discontented with the Duke of Wellington, and is left to worship her own idols and cherish her own prejudices.

Whether, however, either or both of these bills be passed, or be thrown out, of one thing you may be certain,—that there will be no riots, no revolution; but that amid all the triumph and all the lamentation, order will reign supreme and undisturbed, and the year 1836 will begin with legislation in all its forms, just where 1835 left it.

LETTER XLVIII.

National Prejudices—English Aristocracy—Lords and Commoners
— Desdemona — Russia —The Emperor Nicholas—Prussian
Government—Guarantees—Public and Private Law.

London, June 30th, 1835.

I DINED yesterday with Lord ——. In comparison
with some Germans who were speaking French,
I might hold my English for real English. But
I am much more of an Englishman in another
sense; namely, that I do not want to adjust England to a German pattern, although I am perfectly aware of the advantages of our country, and
the defects of many of the institutions of this.
The importance of the English aristocracy appears in quite a different light, when one sees the
walls of their rooms hung with the master-pieces
of Raphael and Titian, than if they were covered
with receipts of the interests of mortgages.
Yet even here are bankrupt noblemen and over-
wealthy commoners, who, like A——, can give
twenty thousand pounds to each of their five sons
as a Christmas-box.

A —— buys several estates after having
ascertained their value; among others he purchases, without bargaining, a very large one

from Lord ———, with everything on it. On taking possession he finds that many things are missing in the dwelling-house, and writes desiring to have them restored; Lord —— answers, that the things belonged to Lady ———, who had taken them with her, and that he did not expect that so rich a man would make so much pother about such trifles. On which A——— replies that he had bought the things, and was astonished at my Lord's wishing to retain property which he had sold. That if all the things were not on the spot within a given time, he would throw up the bargain and sue his Lordship for damages. That he, A———, had become a rich man by attaching importance to trifles; and that perhaps Lord —— had been forced, by a contrary practice, to sell the property of his ancestors. Hereupon a whole waggon full of things arrives. A—— then writes to Lady —— that he would not allow himself to be bullied, but had great pleasure in returning to her everything that she at all valued.

Lady E———, when comparing Grisi with Malibran, remarked that the latter acted Desdemona with exaggeration. I have before expressed the same opinion in my letters from Paris, and certainly Schroeder-Devrient is far superior to her in this character. But it is the fault of the bad *libretto* and the music, that every actress makes Desdemona far less gentle and engaging than Shakspeare drew her.

London, July 1.

I am now, then, at the beginning of another month, and at the end of three more I must return to Germany. Yesterday I looked over fifteen folios of ambassadors' letters—for the most part an unprofitable labour. Another time I sit a whole day over one volume, and I shall certainly not complete what I projected—spite of the compliments I receive on my industry.

I am not so happy as M—— J——, a French lawyer, whom I met yesterday at Mr. H——'s. He wants to understand only one thing, the English courts of justice, and means to go back in a fortnight.

I have met with Germans and Russians here, who extolled the institutions of their respective countries to such a degree, that everything English was made to appear absurd and mischievous in the comparison.

This way of talking is thoroughly revolting to my historical nature: I require, at least, a far more accurate observation, in order to discover how and whence the good or the bad arose; and in what way it is connected with other things. Religious toleration is greater, for example, in Russia than in England; but this by no means proves that the higher civilization of the former country is the sole cause: it proceeds from many considerations which the English also suffer to have their due weight in India, though not in Ireland.

It is difficult to say which nation in Europe

forms the fairest estimate of other nations. The first step certainly is, to understand them, and not to judge before we know ánything about them. In this respect the Germans have hitherto been the most industrious ; but they have often obscured their descriptions by dry pedantry, or shallow affectation of genius. If the French produce more such works as that of Victor Cousin on Prussian Education, nobody will venture to accuse them again of superficiality.

I mentioned the Russians ; they have just learned something from Europe, and many of them already fancy it their vocation to teach Europe.

A Russian education, if not a tyrannical, will certainly be an oblique one ; something in the style in which they harness the two horses in their droschkas, one quite awry ; which barbarism is as little worthy to be imitated in Berlin as other Russian fashions. The French ultra-liberalism, and the Russian absolutism, are two dishes offered gratis, which a rational German will equally reject, without affecting to impose his own fare on the two *restaurateurs de l'Europe.*

In one respect, however, the Russians are far happier than many of the nations of Europe. They have a constitution suited to their wants. A constitution ! you exclaim ; they have no constitution at all ! They have, I grant, no Chambers, no elections, no right and left side, no *tiers parti,* no right and left centre ; but they have, what politics require, no less than mathematics, they have *a* centre ; and that is the Emperor.

A deliberating and debating body, a general code, an equal church for the whole Russian empire, with all its tribes—all this were senseless and impracticable. The *forms* of older and more homogeneous states are perfectly inapplicable to this pattern card of nations, religions, degrees of civilization, &c.

They want *a man* to direct the whole, and their emperor is a man, in the full sense of the word, body and soul. In him great qualities for dominion are unquestionably combined; an imposing yet attractive exterior, admirable activity, a rare strength of will, and dauntless courage. These were the qualities which gave him the crown in a moment of the greatest peril; and the manner in which he subdued that peril rendered him worthy to wear it.

But the last approving or condemning judgment will be pronounced by history, when it is known whether he uniformly respected the rights of independent states, and esteemed their amity more valuable than their subjection.

A merely personal guarantee is certainly always more or less dependent on the life of the warrantor. However, the constitution of the Emperor Nicholas seems to me of such a sort, that I would rather have an annuity on his life than on that of many a paper constitution.

No policy should, or indeed can, be founded on personal qualities alone, because they are all subject to a thousand influences. People often ask me here, Who can guarantee you Prussians against a total overthrow of your admirable and liberal institutions whenever the king dies ?

I might answer, his successor; because I know that, with a head and a heart like his, such a revulsion is impossible. But, granting that a king of Prussia were to arise who knew nothing of his people, or of his age, and that he conceived the arbitrary project of forcibly introducing the character of another people and another period, it were utterly impossible. We trust in persons, but we trust in things too.

It is therefore impossible to restore the closed ·gates, the internal duties, the villenage, the recruiting and flogging, the duty-labour, the tithes, &c.; or to abolish religious toleration, the schools, and the universities. The bright and the dark side of the old and of the new may be examined, developed, reformed; but there will be no revolution, backward or forward.

On this point (as I have lately experienced) the idea of Right, regulating in appearance, but often confusing in reality, is urged. Scarcely has less evil been inflicted under the plea of right than under that of force. Does not indeed the frequent repetition of the maxim, "*fiat justitia pereat mundus*," prove that the spirit of justice is entirely misunderstood, and the letter only attended to? True justice sustains the world; it is the breath of the living, not the grave of the dead. At first this absurd dream arose out of the false notion that Right only preserved its character by constant uniformity and immobility. People forgot that the high office of legislation would then be utterly annihilated, and that nothing would remain but the application and administration of law.

The second grand error, (of which I have so often had occasion to speak) is the absolute supremacy which public law arrogates over private, or private over public. Strange—that not a few champions of the German institutions of the Middle Ages (when it serves their turn) seek to apply to them the absolute private law of the times of the Roman emperors; although this was wholly incompatible with the stirring political life of the infamy of modern Europe. This is connected with the fables of Herr von Haller, who wants us to believe that at that time, or at some time, the state arose out of nothing, and consisted of nothing but the sum total of innumerable little contracts which moved about, *ad libitum*, like Epicurus's atoms, and thus effected all the wonders of the development of the human race. He and his disciples see light solely in the existence and maintenance of this atomistic confusion, and concede to the caprice of any body establishing anything, unlimited power to all eternity. According to them, if a worshipper of Venus *vulgivaga* founded a temple in her honour two thousand years ago, it would be an unjust violation of his will to convert it into a Christian school. This sounds ridiculous and monstrous. But is it less ridiculous if, as I am told, Greek must be unalterably taught by a certain grammar in some schools here, because that is the will of the founder; though that grammar, which was the best in his time, is the worst now? Is it less foolish and pitiful to demand compensation for every slight loss consequent upon new laws, and to drop all consideration of the enormous gain of the new impulse to civilization?

Every year—nay every day and every hour—produces some change in me and in my powers and my rights. If I lose the blossoms of youth, I gain the fruits of mature manhood; and if I overlook this compensation, I fall into useless, unnatural lamentations. A generation which throws off all reverence for its forefathers will take no root, and will be thrown aside in its turn—as the events of the French Revolution sufficiently proved. A generation which looks backward in search of all help and all instruction will, like Lot's wife, lose all sense and motion.

I write a great many variations upon the same grand theme; but my life here constantly leads me into these reflections: have patience, and indulgence, therefore, and kindly accept what each day brings forth.

END OF VOL. II.

CPSIA information can be obtained
at www.ICGtesting.com
Printed in the USA
BVHW090737081118
532427BV00011B/300/P